BEEP!
BEEP!

BEEP! BEEP!

COMPETING IN THE AGE OF THE ROAD RUNNER

CHIP R. BELL & OREN HARARI

WARNER BOOKS

A Time Warner Company

Copyright © 2000 by Warner Brothers, Chip R. Bell and Oren Harari
All rights reserved.
Warner Books, Inc., 1271 Avenue of the Americas,
New York, NY 10020
Visit our Web site at www.twbookmark.com

 A Time Warner Company

Printed in the United States of America
First Warner Books Printing: February 2000
10 9 8 7 6 5 4 3 2 1

Library of Congress Cataloging-in-Publication Data

Bell, Chip R.
    Beep beep : competing in the age of the Road Runner / Chip R.
Bell and Oren Harari.
        p.   cm.
    Includes index.
    ISBN 0-446-52353-4
    1. Executive ability.   2. Industrial management.   I. Harari,
Oren.   II. Title.
HD38.2.B445   2000
658.4'09—dc21   99-30164
                                                                          CIP

Book design and composition by L&G McRee

Dedicated to:

Bilijack Ray Bell
Jordan Liam Harari
Dylan Samuel Harari

Road Runners of the New Millennium

CONTENTS

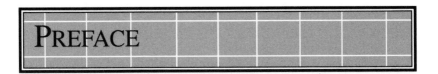

PREFACE

Road Runners don't have prefaces . . . they just begin!

BEEP!
BEEP!

CHAPTER 1

"And in This Corner, Weighing Twenty-three Pounds . . ."

Two cartoon characters meet on the New Mexico desert to match wits. Spectators are instantly struck by the David and Goliath parallel. The program that came with the tickets says that coyotes can run thirty miles per hour . . . and this particular coyote is hungry, already tasting his next meal. And it tells us that roadrunners can't really fly—soaring short distances is about it—and can run sixteen miles per hour . . . tops.

Wile E. Coyote brings several other advantages to the fray. He has a seemingly endless arsenal of roadrunner-trapping gadgets, provided by a mysterious manufacturer named Acme. And he relentlessly uses these tools against his scrawny, defenseless opponent with great cunning and stealth. He is a master planner, obsessed with visions of fricasseed roadrunner!

1

The line on this match heavily favors the Coyote. Who would bet a dime on the multicolored, gawky bird who seems oblivious to the fact that a contest is even underway? Yet time and again, the Road Runner eludes and escapes! As we toss the stubs of our betting slips, the Road Runner's victories baffle us.

The Road Runner's feats defy logic. He races through imaginary tunnels as if they were real. He never gets wet when there's water everywhere. He outmaneuvers a faster, stronger opponent by making speed superfluous. He turns the ingenuity of his opponent into embarrassing results . . . so embarrassing that spectators laugh, even though they bet on the Coyote. How can we comprehend such absurdity?

The Road Runner has a secret that Wile E. never figures out. He is operating under completely different rules. He understands what Albert Einstein once said: "You can't solve the problems of a paradigm from within the paradigm."

This book is about the Road Runner paradigm. Wile E. can't even pronounce *paradigm*, much less understand that as long as he clings to an outmoded set of assumptions to guide his plans and actions, he cannot avoid the blunders and errors that doom him to perpetual hunger.

A paradigm is a way of viewing the world—like Newton vs. Einstein or Ptolemy vs. Copernicus. You remember from school days studying about the lengths people will go to hold on to their favorite worldview. When nature did not fit the "Earth is the center of the universe" paradigm of Ptolemy's day, astronomers added a fudge factor called epicycles to make it work. Like Wile E., they worked harder to protect conventional wisdom than to give it up. Ptolemys are still out there in full force today.

Success in this new millennium requires a completely new way of managing ourselves and our enterprises. The rules of the road have changed and we must master them quickly if our businesses and our lives are to be successful—and fun. Solving future challenges with present-day patterns will be as futile as the Acme schemes on which Wile E. relies. It's like

2

trying to solve a Zen koan with Western logic (" . . . so, what *is* the sound of one hand clapping?"). Like Wile E., we scratch our heads in confusion, even after we hear the answer. It isn't that Wile E. doesn't *know* that he loses; he doesn't *understand* why he loses! Our hope is that you'll be ready for the riddles of the new millennium by the time you've read the last word on the last page.

Bugs into Bulldozers:
Surviving Managers Are Transformers

When a young child was asked to explain why he liked the transformer toys that were the current rage, he said, "They're neat! If I have a plain old toy car I might be able to take stuff off of it and make it a hot rod. But with a transformer, I can turn a bug into a bulldozer!" We believe that the next few years will have us wanting fewer "ordinary cars that can become hot rods" and wanting more "bugs that can be transformed into bulldozers."

The world of enterprise often attempts to operate in a Porsche world with buggy whip thinking. Many "truths" that now are albatrosses around the necks of new millennium pioneers are vestiges of an irrelevant past. It's like public schools still closing for the summer fifty years after the end of the agricultural era. Or, it's like . . .

- "Managing" employees by command and control and behind closed doors.
- Dealing with suppliers in an arm's-length, adversarial, hyper-legalistic manner.
- Assuming that gradual changes to the status quo are less risky than going for breakthroughs.
- Assuming your most valuable assets are the tangible ones that show up on the balance sheet.
- Defining your organization or unit in terms of real es-

3

tate and location rather than global networks and relationships.

- Seeing salvation in mass markets, cost effectiveness, and economies of scale, rather than in perpetually innovative solutions for market units of one (i.e., each customer).
- Clinging to the belief that "mating" with another coyote company will somehow yield a roadrunner organization.

The patterns, paradigms, and rules practiced in today's world of management and leadership have a long and rich history. And they once worked! But no more . . . take it from Hewlett-Packard CEO Lew Platt: "Whatever made you successful in the past won't in the future."

As we move into the new millennium, we face completely new business realities, requiring completely new management mind-sets and leadership models. The winners in this era will be the nimble, mobile organizations that can, on a dime, gather and shed diverse constituents whose loyalties are less to the current concoction and more to their own competencies and talents. Free-agent mercenaries will be in; gold watches, out. Independent proprietors will be in; subordinates, out. New realities call for new paradigms.

Enter . . . the Road Runner! The Road Runner is unencumbered by mass and fat (and meetings, and sign-off approvals, and huge sunk costs, and politicking). He is the essence of versatility, ingenuity, turn-on-a-dime agility, zigzag mind-set, and sheer joy. The Coyote relies on a ploddingly predictable set of tactics and style of execution—including his dependence on one of the most inept suppliers imaginable. He's stuck in a rut, which invariably costs him his meal . . . and his pride.

4

A Map for the Millennium

The contrasts between roadrunners and coyotes are most instructive for leaders who seek a map for maneuvering in the new millennium. If you look at the Spirit of the Road Runner as a desired effect or result, what is the process for achieving it? Stated differently, if you wanted your organization or unit to be a roadrunner among coyotes, if you wanted all your employees to act more like roadrunners and less like coyotes, what actions would you take as a leader?

Beep Beep is about bringing a new spirit to the work world. It is intended as a practical blueprint and a courage-builder for business pioneers who are unwilling to be lulled into complacence by the latest Acme trick or fooled by a painted tunnel. The book is designed to be your periscope for envisioning the future and a guidebook to ready you for the trip from here to there. It is a working book—one aimed at being more edgy than conventional, more vivacious than staid, more sensible than scholarly—and much more about practice than philosophy.

It's important to emphasize that *Beep Beep* is not a simple homage to small companies. There are many little coyotes out there—small companies or units that are slow in decision-making, ponderous in market response, ruled by a dictator, behind in technology, and just plain uninteresting in the products and services they offer. The issue is not big vs. small. In the Age of Road Runner, the issue is, which species are you striving to be? The key question this book seeks to answer is: How can I help my team, unit, or organization become a roadrunner?

This book will show you how to prepare for—and succeed—in the Age of the Road Runner. But beware! The Road Runner himself is giving us a very important clue—and warning—that we must heed before getting on the racetrack to our future. Review these two scenes and guess the clue he gives us.

5

Wile E. holds a medicine bottle. A tight shot on the label reveals its contents: "Acme Hi-Speed Tonic—Contains vitamins R-P+M." He gives a spoonful to a small mouse, who runs around at turbo speed. Wile E. then drinks the whole bottle and jets off turbo speed in pursuit of the Road Runner. The Road Runner suddenly stops, extends his foot, and trips Wile E., who goes tumbling into a construction zone and into a small shed with a door sign, "Danger. Dynamite. Keep Out." The shed explodes, sending Wile E. through the chimney and into space.

The scene opens with a close shot on a box labeled: "One Acme Jet Propelled Pogo Stick." Wile E. removes the pogo stick, starts it up, mounts it, and waits for the Road Runner to run by. As the Road Runner races by, Wile E. starts pogoing up and down in hot pursuit. But he soon loses control of the pogo stick and goes straight backward over a cliff.

What these scenes show is that you cannot remain a coyote and expect to compete against roadrunners by simply copying their movements. Sure, the coyote can buy high-speed tonic or jet-propelled pogo sticks, but his body and soul are still coyote. If you are a coyote team or organization, no matter what fads or quick fixes you jump into, you are just imitating a roadrunner—and the real thing will beat you every time. In this book, we'll help you learn to be the real thing.

Sometimes we will be focusing on roadrunner organizations, sometimes on roadrunner leaders. Success comes through embodying the Spirit of the Road Runner, whether that application is to a person, a team, or an entire organization. The cartoon characters created by Chuck Jones are both male. But we approach the *concepts* of roadrunner and coyote as gender-free. Likewise we will refer to the cartoon characters by their proper names: Wile E. Coyote and Road Runner. We will refer to the concepts in lower case.

Take a Closer Look

Wile E. Coyote is preoccupied, earnest, conniving, and grim. The Road Runner is joyful, light, and free. Wile E. does nothing but go from pursuing one meal to the next, with perpetual frustration; the bird is gleefully living life to the fullest. The results are always the same: Wile E. somehow manages to dig himself into the hole of failure, while the Road Runner strides on, undeterred and unaffected by life's bumps and obstacles.

Are you a coyote? Or are you a roadrunner? And how about your organization? We all like to think we're roadrunners. The truth is most of us are not. After all, the coyote way has worked for years. In the coyote world, solid professional management means being persistent and focused. Coyotes are lean and mean—especially "mean." Coyotes develop a smart idea or great plan . . . then ruthlessly obsess on execution, never deviating from the plan until they reach the last step. Coyotes never give up or stray from the course. Sounds reasonable, doesn't it?

Coyote thinking has worked in the past. But supervisors, managers, and executives, if pushed to be candid, will confess that in the last few years the old formulas for success are beginning to feel wobbly. Pressing the pedal harder only spins our wheels in place, maybe even digging us in deeper.

Too many of our goals seem unreachable, the pace seems too fast to negotiate the steep slope ahead. It feels like we've bought a bill of goods—perhaps from the Acme Company. We got the right degrees from the right schools, paid our dues, and kept our noses clean, yet now watch raw, unrefined upstarts (sometimes college dropouts) outdo us by redoing the rules. What do these mavericks know that we don't?

As we watch the cartoons, there are many reasons we admire the Road Runner. He's a free spirit, marching to his own drum above the mundane, minute, and meticulous. He's light, joyful, and seemingly fearless. He's fast, bouncy, and always looking ahead. And he's garbed in glorious color, not dull like the Coyote. It's somehow much easier to imagine Wile E. in a drab three-piece suit than the Road Runner.

We have mixed feelings about Wile E. Coyote. He's true to his name—"Wile E."—as in sly, cunning, clever, crafty . . . wily. We admire his tenacity and endurance; yet we disdain his dark side. There's an appealing curiosity in him in a sinister sort of way. But he's way too myopically obsessed . . . which leads to narrow vision and appallingly poor execution. We appreciate his ingenuity. Yet he operates out of such a small, narrow picture of the world that he's unable to adjust to his environment. His goals are winner take all—he wants to kill and eat the competition—literally. He defines the game as win-lose and, ironically, becomes the loser.

Scene opens on an Acme Street Wagon, a 500-pound anvil, a self-inflating weather balloon, and an electric fan. Wile E. stands in the wagon, which is attached to the balloon, anvil tied to one side, fan on the other. He checks the contraption over and turns on the fan. The fan propels him over the edge of the cliff. As he flies smirking through the air, he spies the Road Runner through the clouds, zooming along the road. He unties the anvil and drops it over the side. The sudden loss of weight causes the balloon to shoot up. Then the tie holding the balloon begins to unravel, causing the balloon to release its air and jerk around wildly. Finally, all the air is out of the balloon, Wile E. falls, passing the anvil on the way down, and crashes onto the road. The anvil falls on his head. The Road Runner runs over the anvil.

Thinking of trying a middle ground? Forget it. It's impossible to be a blend of Wile E. and the Road Runner. You might alternate from one persona to the other, but you can never be both at once. Biologically and organizationally, the two will never merge . . . there will never be a Wile E. Roadrunner! Taking the moderate, safe route in search of a hybrid not only produces deformed offspring like the mule; it leads to sterility and extinction.

The Origin of the Chase

The Road Runner and Wile E. Coyote were born on September 16, 1949, in a cartoon titled *Fast and Furry-ous*, the creation of Warner Bros. cartoonist Charles Martin "Chuck" Jones. "The Road Runner seemed funny— a bird that runs," wrote Jones in his autobiography, *Chuck Amuck*. "They're like flying fish of the land. And the Coyote, by his very nature, is never well-fed—he's always hungry. So you don't have to explain it. You come across a coyote chasing a roadrunner—he'd chase anything."

Jones chose the name Acme Corporation as Wile E.'s sole supplier because, as he describes in his autobiography, "My sister Dorothy fell in love with the title Acme, finding it was adopted by many struggling and embryonic companies because it put them close to the top of their chosen services in the Yellow Pages. Acme and Wile E. were the perfect symbiotic relationship; whatever his needs were, Acme was there to supply. No money was ever involved."

Jones established a framework for the Road Runner cartoons that gave them resilience and coherence. In his book he outlines some of the boundaries.

- No outside force can harm the Coyote—only his own ineptitude or the failure of the Acme products. Whenever possible, make gravity the Coyote's greatest enemy.

- The Coyote could stop anytime—if he were not a fanatic.

- The only dialogue is "Beep Beep."

- The Coyote is never to be injured by the Road Runner.

- The cartoons are always seen from the point of view of the Coyote.

CHAPTER 2

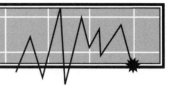

Competing in the Terrain
of the Future

The group of sales reps from a large aftermarket parts distributor gathered in a ballroom for the start of their annual sales rally. Excited to get their brand-new four-inch-thick parts and price book, they largely ignored the CEO as he highlighted the company's previous year wins and losses.

Then the meeting took an unexpected turn. The CEO introduced the opening keynote speaker . . . a business consultant who had entertained the audience the previous year. But instead of opening with the expected clever joke, he walked in their midst and changed their view of their future with three questions:

> If all your customers could at any time remotely "look" into your warehouse, find the solution or part they needed, and get it shipped overnight, what would they need you for?

> If all your products were engineered to be "smart," and the part itself could alert the distribution center when it needed to be changed, replenished, or deleted, what would your customers need you for?

If all price shopping was driven by real-time, global comparisons via the Internet and customers could request customized products and services which in turn drove your production cycles, what would they need you for?

The terrain of the future will be dramatically different from anything we have had in the past. The Internet is both a part of the change as well as a cultural symbol of that change. The Internet is the ultimate roadrunner terrain. Coyotes are simply lost in this bizarre environment. All their size, girth, marketing muscle, and economies of scale help little in a world where nothing is fixed, stable, predictable, or tangible, and where everything proceeds with nonlinear warp speed.

Chip Valentine understands. Chip is the past president of the National Welding Supply Association, which represents distributors of industrial gas and related supplies. In a keynote speech to the national meeting of the association in late 1998, he pointed out a truism that applies to every industry, mainly, that "new forces are going to dramatically change the way we will do business in the twenty-first century." And what are those new forces? "The Internet, and electronic commerce in general," he told the audience, "have had little effect on us until now, but they will have a tremendous impact on us over the next few years. Those of us who have dabbled in it have seen it as a small competitive advantage maybe, but it will soon be a requirement to do business." Global traffic over the Internet doubles every 100 days with 60,000 new people logging on every day in the U.S. alone.

Valentine went on to give an intriguing example, citing a fellow member of the association's board: "Ed lives in northern Wisconsin and grocery shopping is very inconvenient, especially in the winter. His wife recently placed an order for groceries at www.netgrocer.com. The selection was wonderful, the prices were better than at the local grocery store, and they were delivered right to her door by UPS—for a $2.99 delivery charge. Ed's question to the board was, 'If this works so well with groceries, can www.weldingsupplies.com be far behind?'"

This is the vital question for grocers as well as welding suppliers. A slow unexciting grocery chain that simply opens a Web site (or merges with another slow, unexciting grocery chain to produce an even bigger, slower offspring) won't survive. That's coyotes trying to imitate roadrunners. E-commerce, to paraphrase Valentine, is more than a dabble, more than an offshoot of the current business, more than simply providing employees with PCs, more than simply using EDI to link up with suppliers. The real question is how do you capitalize on the new realities of the Internet in order to reinvent your business? If you're a grocer, what's the grocery business going to look like tomorrow? Will there be "stores" the way we know them? Will there be "stores" at all? And how do you use the tools and highways of electronic commerce to make these transformations to do what seems impossible today?

Nowadays, the Road Runner thrives in *any* environment, but he positively *dominates* in a digital terrain. Writing in *Fast Company*, founding editor Alan Webber notes: "In the past, competing on time created performance differentials. But as real as those differentials were, they usually improved things only 20% or 30%. When you move into the digital world, you attach a supercharger to speed as a competitive weapon. The difference between those who get it and those who don't is no longer incremental—it's a quantum leap. And once that disparity becomes apparent to some consumers, word spreads to others."

But, again, keep in mind that the move to the Internet and digital economy is not simply about buying gee-whiz technology (the Coyote is always buying gee-whiz technology from Acme). It's more about organizational metamorphosis—toward quantum leaps in roadrunner-like speed, fluidity, lightness, responsiveness, precision, and agility. That's why the next-wave strategies of Dell Computer and Cisco Systems, two of the most successful companies in the 1990s, now revolve almost entirely around the Internet: selling on it, customizing product on it, communicating one-on-one with customers on it, providing after-sale servicing on it, partnering and outsourcing on it, allowing customers to take care of their own questions and problems on it—all instantaneously, real-time, individualized, on "customer-time."

The reality of the Age of the Road Runner is that winning teams and organizations will not be able to capitalize on what were core elements of businesses of the past. Organizing around sacred cow principles of secrets, security, allegiance, time, place, order, or supremacy will be a prescription for extinction in the Age of the Road Runner. Here are the realities of the new environment of business:

No More Secrets

The desert is the terrain of the Road Runner–Wile E. Coyote cartoons, and it is the turf of our future. It is a stark setting: a bare-bones, inhospitable, brutally hot expanse. Unfortunately, we're more accustomed to a jungle-like business landscape (as in "It's a jungle out there!"), where the heavy entanglements of secrecy, the thick fog of politicking, and the dense underbrush of buck-passing obscure your vision and block the path. The desert, in contrast, is clean, wide, open. For the Road Runner, the desert offers clear-cut opportunities and barrier-free paths to success. The desert's purity and clarity reek of Road Runner–type honesty . . . with no BS and few places to hide (though Wile E. pathetically tries to, over and over).

The desert in which tomorrow's organizations will operate offers similar mixed blessings. There's no hiding behind excuses, closed doors, policies, or hierarchical levels. No Adam and Eve paradise here, with lush low-hanging fruit, fat cats, cash cows, and steady streams of income. The organizational desert is open—information technology and flattened structures give access to competitive knowledge to anyone, anywhere, anytime. For roadrunner organizations, the new desert is alive with opportunity. However, for coyote organizations, which rely on secrecy, stealth, one-upmanship, and power plays, the business landscape of tomorrow will be a nightmare.

The desert is open, and it calls for open responses. Wile E. doesn't quite get that. His first name is synonymous with trickery and deception! Almost every Road Runner–Wile E. Coyote script begins with a secret plan—a devious scheme to snare the little bird. His tricks epitomize deceit. They are carried out with great reliance on covertness and stealth.

The business world has had a long-standing love affair with secrecy and stealth. Corporate espionage, insider trading, and paper shredders have littered the landscape of enterprise. Elaborate security systems are the hallmark of corporate headquarters buildings. "Confidential" is a well-used rubber stamp. Managers get private briefings after reading numbered copies of classified reports. And that's just the beginning. On a daily basis, coyote organizations chug along fueled by political secrets, back stabbings, "for your eyes only," "can't-share-that-stuff" mentality, everyone in their box, and closed-door whisperings. That world will be inappropriate and unsustainable in the twenty-first century.

Today, technology universalizes and democratizes information. The management of governments, corporations, hospitals, and unions—you name it—can no longer keep information under wraps. You need advice about a physician, a hospital, a surgical procedure, a disease, a medication? Click on a mouse and you're immediately connected to the world's knowledge bank. You need the lowest prices and optimum features for cars, long-distance services, or mortgage rates? You want the real story about a potential product or a potential supplier? Click on a mouse and you're immediately connected to the world's knowledge bank. You see a need to reduce the time between customer orders and your company's delivery of the product? Click on a mouse and you get real-time information about inventory control, logistics, current costs, the impact of delivery time on cash flow, and the impact of the current order cycle on customer satisfaction.

"As globalization gives everyone the same information, resources, technology and markets," says *New York Times* political writer Thomas Friedman, "a society's particular ability to put those pieces together in the fastest and most innovative manner increasingly separates winners from losers in the global economy." The same goes for business units and organizations. Information is free and ubiquitous. This is why roadrunner organizations capitalize on openness, for they know it's not the information and data that are crucial but what smart, creative people do with it. So their credo is: no secrets, spread information everywhere. Like Dorothy with the Wizard of Oz, they lift up the curtains. In contrast to their coyote competitors, they work "out in the open" as much as possible.

We live in an open world but still tend to operate as if it were closed. Yet children routinely fire up home computers more powerful than the Cray Supercomputers used by the Strategic Air Command thirty years ago. Teenagers use the Internet to access any data on the planet for their term papers. But in our coyote organizations adult employees are still denied unrestricted, unfiltered contact with sensitive data. Customers and outsiders (analysts, consultants, vendors) can often "see" more of an organization (its processes, its financials, its inventory, its strategic priorities) than employees can. People read about your organization in the paper; the world may know more about it than you.

Coyote thinking is about hoarding and protecting information, about power and cash cows. Roadrunner thinking is getting information out. It says, "Let's spread information everywhere so everyone can be stronger and more effective." "Let's obsolete ourselves before someone else does." "Information grows old fast, so why hoard it?" Instead, roadrunner energy goes into the next—not the last—product, service, idea. Wile E. secretly protects what he does. The Road Runner is not concerned about that. He roars all over the desert, looking ahead, free to absorb everything around him.

No More Security

We are all a little ambivalent about security. At some level, we know it's false. We laugh at Wile E.'s dilemma because we so often fall into the same trap he does. Security implies protection, predictability, exterior reliability, a sense of peace—the feeling that "someone else is taking care of me." Wile E. seeks the security of a sole-source supplier . . . Acme. He seeks the security of the instructions on the box: Do X, Y, and Z as instructed and the bird is yours! Despite his perpetual disappointment, he clings to the same modus operandi, the same strategic plan, over and over . . . and when it doesn't work, he redoubles his effort (like "continuous improvement") and tries the same MO with a different ruse.

The victorious Road Runner's well-being doesn't depend on anyone else; he uses any resource out there—especially his own capabilities. He doesn't look back to what he did yesterday when dealing with today's situation. His is a true sense of security, a self-assurance that inner peace comes from self-reliance, not other-reliance.

As we shall see, the Road Runner periodically reaches out to "allies"—but the Road Runner does not compulsively call on external organizations or quick-fix techniques for help—unlike Wile E., who clings to them. Wile E. wastes his energy choosing and trying all kinds of outlandish props—from dehydrated rocks to rocket skates—hoping they will guarantee him success. He doesn't even test-drive his strategies; he puts them to use straight out of the Acme carton.

What do roadrunners do? They think differently. Consider this: If your organization spun you off as a subsidiary with your own profit and loss statement and required you to justify your presence by the impact you made, who would be your customers and what would they be willing to pay for your efforts? Guess what! You already *have* been spun off! The Wile E.'s don't know it and continue to act entitled; Road Runners already view their departments as profit centers, their divisions as unique businesses, and themselves as their

17

own company. They have turned themselves into Me, Inc., and are busily marketing and delivering their services to others.

Coyotes assume that outside forces (like employers or benign corporations) will offer them security. Then they are crushed when they don't get the promotion they expected, or even worse, when they become a downsize statistic. Even when they keep their job, they often find themselves in a constant state of low-level anxiety about their future in the organization.

Roadrunners (individuals and organizations) create their own security. They focus on being different, continually learning, taking important risks, and making a difference every day—making themselves more indispensable to their current organization and more marketable to others.

No More Allegiance

Wile E. Coyote loves Acme! Boy oh boy, does he love Acme! He buys and buys and buys. Check out his account history with Acme:

Account Name: Mr. Wile E. Coyote

Address: Somewhere on the Run, New Mexico

Re: Products Purchased to Date

- Small canister of Acme Aspirin
- Acme Rocket Powered Roller Skates
- One "Acme Super Outfit"—blue body suit, red cape, yellow socks and gloves, mask
- One sheet of Acme Triple Strength Battleship Steel Armor Plate
- One Acme Batman's Outfit
- From Acme Anvil Corp: Contents: One (1) Anvil
- Acme Giant Rubber Band
- Acme Street Wagon, 500-pound Anvil, Weather Balloon (self-inflating type), Electric Fan

- Acme Mouse Snare
- One Bottle of Acme Hi-Speed Tonic—Contains vitamins R–P+M
- One Acme Jet Propelled Pogo Stick
- One Acme Jet Propelled Unicycle (satisfaction guaranteed)
- One Acme Female Road-Runner Costume
- One Jim-Dandy Wagon, One Acme Outboard Motor
- Acme Iron Pellets
- One Fifth of Acme Bumblebees
- Acme Axle Grease—Guaranteed Slippery

Wile E. sticks with Acme, despite his never-ending disappointment. He probably calls their toll-free number repeatedly, credit card in hand, like some forlorn lover. Wile E.'s in love with Acme all right, but he's even more infatuated with the process that controls him, that drives his actions, his attitudes, and his results. His first love is a blinding, driving goal—EAT THE BIRD. This means stealth, deceit, and Acme . . . over and over and over. Never is he successful—or happy—but he is a faithful customer even though Acme never acknowledges his existence. Acme never follows up. There are no customized solutions, no requests for feedback, no sales rep visits, and no sense of partnership. And so the Coyote's allegiance exacerbates his myopia, rigidity, and possessive holding on to old tools, perspectives, and attitudes.

The Road Runner is not tied down to one product line, vendor, institution, organization, process, or set of instructions. He is loyal to his ethics, his purpose, his goals, his principles, his environment, and himself. The Road Runner avoids the Coyote's shortcomings . . . no false pride, no arrogance, no unrealistic expectations. The Road Runner chooses his attitude: optimistic self-reliance. The Coyote allows his attitude to rule him: He lets himself be a victim of external circumstance, and the circumstance renders him gloomy, obediently dependent, blindly allegiant.

Blind allegiance is the hallmark of security-driven organizations and employees. In time this "taking for granted" allegiance becomes self-righteous, self-absorbed, and self-defeating. Allegiance is no longer enough, as Intel is now telling its suppliers: If you want to keep our business, don't just respond to our directives. Take the lead, take the initiative; get involved in our operations, suggest things you can provide that will help both our strategic objectives, show us that you understand our business and can help us improve it. If you do that, you'll stay part of our family even though the life of the original project we hired you for will have ended. In other words, don't count on us to show allegiance to you just because you've been our vendor for a thousand years, or just because you meet the terms of the contract with zero defects. We're not interested in commodity services or commodity transactions. That's not enough. Partner with us to add value to our business in new, fresh ways, and we'll be loyal to you.

Allegiance is not the same as loyalty or commitment. We choose to be loyal or committed to someone or something; we are obliged to allegiance. Roadrunners demonstrate loyalty. Blind, binding allegiance is reserved for coyotes and their canine cousins, not smart organizations and leaders.

No More Time

We all learned in Philosophy 101 that time doesn't really exist . . . it's just a convenient convention, concocted eons ago to make life predictable. In many ways, the concept of business time is under radical overhaul. Winning organizations are sure to be those that use time (or the lack of it) as their ally.

The 1980s and 1990s focused on creating a just-in-time world. Raw materials were no longer stockpiled days or months before their use in the manufacturing process. Since carrying costs were soaring, most product makers learned how to minimize holding time for inventory. This concept was amplified by the concept of cycle time, the through-put time of manufacturing. Given narrowing margins and the fact that goods in production were a drain on the expense side of the equation, factories scrambled to find ways to shorten the time between the purchase of raw materials and the shipment of finished goods.

All organizations now focus on compressing time . . . speeding up their responses and processes, making things happen faster and faster. Pick up a phone or turn on your laptop and, like magic, time seems to disappear. You're connected to any piece of information, to anyone, anywhere. Technology squeezes time to irrelevance. It's all "real-time" now.

When people think about the Road Runner, they usually think first of speed. And it's certainly true that roadrunner organizations look at compressing time as a vital competitive advantage: speed up time to market, responsiveness to customers, buildups of electronic networks, reactions to market trends. FedEx's remarkable ability to track instantaneously (indeed, its ability to allow the customer to track instantaneously) the precise location of any en-route parcel is a key competitive advantage. So is Disney's capacity to churn out a new entertainment product—a movie, a game, a videotape, a toy—every five minutes. As Dayton Hudson chairman Bob Ulrich tells his managers: "Speed is life."

For the past few years, Professor Bill Murray, one of Oren's colleagues at the University of San Francisco, has held an annual eight-week seminar with leaders from a variety of European companies. Shortly after the stock price of Yahoo! took one of the periodic big leaps, Bill told Oren something interesting. His European clients have no problem understanding a market valuation of a billion dollars for an Internet-based company, nor do they have a problem understanding how any American start-up can raise millions and then be worth billions. What they can't understand is the speed with which it happens! How can people take a concept, raise capital, form an organization, set up supplier links, form global networks, market and sell their wares, and be appraised at huge multiples of earnings so quickly? How do they get the people, train them, get them the tools and technology they need, create plans and systems and processes under which they will work—so quickly?

For these international executives (and for many domestic American ones as well) the image of people choosing to work fifteen hours a day in ad hoc, ambiguous "organizations" with very loose job expectations, then collapsing in a sleeping bag under their desks when they get tired—at any hour of the day—in order to create a shared dream and gain access to millions in stock options is an alien concept. These skeptics still see business development in terms of slow, deliberate planning and execution. They still see work in terms of a compartmentalized nine-to-five, forty-hour-a-week schedule (and for some, that's a heavy week). They still view financial rewards in terms of straight, fixed salaries. In a world populated only by coyotes, all that is eminently reasonable. But when the stage is shared by roadrunners, those premises go right out the window.

Coyote managers and organizations are held prisoner by speed barriers that they create: a maze of holy structures and processes, sacred hierarchical levels and pass-offs, centralized decision-making, trickle-down communication flows, always-done-it-this-way traditions, meticulous planning sessions, political massaging, perpetual committee meetings and reviews, more paper trails and proposals, wait-for-the-other-guy attitudes, arm's-length relationships with outsiders, technologies that are "cost-effective" but out of date, cultures that value convention over experimentation, and hyper-caution over risk.

The Road Runner simply has no time for such stuff! The Road Runner's world is not just about speed; it's also about anticipation, responsiveness, imagination, and—most of all—*agility*. Speed is about pace; agility is about nimbleness. If the Road Runner were simply fast, it wouldn't be enough. If he took the same routes and showed up at the expected times, he'd eventually be caught. The key to the Road Runner's success is that he's more than just fast. He's unpredictable, he zigs and zags, he reacts creatively real-time. In a world where linear speed is a commodity, any organization can use technologies that compress time. The key is this: What do you *do* with those technologies? What can you create that is different, unique, or special? In a world where speed is a commodity, being fast equals no more than surviving. The key to thriving is no longer just the ability to work fast, but *what* you are able to do fast.

Even on a personal level, time is no longer the overriding principle. The Road Runner doesn't know or care if it is 8:00 A.M. or 5:00 P.M. or if it's Tuesday or Saturday. Human roadrunners may declare that Thursday and Friday are going to be the weekend this week and it'll be Tuesday and Wednesday next week. This isn't the orientation of a lazy person. Nor are we talking about the "super woman" ostentatiously juggling twenty-five things at work and home simultaneously, or the workaholic businessman receiving an e-mail at his hotel saying, "Congratulations, it's a boy!" Those are simply images of coyotes trying to imitate roadrunners.

The Road Runner knows that we are entering an age when, once again, distinctions between work and "life" are becoming meaningless. Increasingly, in roadrunner organizations, we can choose when to work and when not to. Individuals brave enough to create a "no-time" mind-set will win, personally and professionally. Organizations that can create a "no-time" culture will be able to attract and mobilize people who choose not to be bound by the clock—aka the roadrunners.

Finally, "no more time" is an interesting play on words. Roadrunner leaders behave as if there is no more time. They have a sense of urgency to take action and try things out. They have an understanding that if they don't act boldly now they will be left behind. They fully understand AB Investor Chairman Percy Barnevik's warning that "nowadays, the cost of delays exceeds the cost of mistakes."

No More Place

Where does the Road Runner live? Apparently, he has no address. Wile E. Coyote, however, must have a permanent headquarters—otherwise where would Acme keep mailing him all the stuff he orders?

For the Road Runner, "place" is irrelevant to getting the job done. Energy devoted to "place thinking" is energy that could be devoted to results. The advent of telecommuting, satellite employees, intranets, outsourcing, contract work, mobility work on the customer's or distributor's or other department's site—all make "place" an unimportant part of enterprise. The "place" of the future is not bolted to the ground. It is virtually anywhere.

Sun Microsystems, located in the heart of Silicon Valley, California, relies heavily on the work of their chief technologist Bill Joy—who lives in Aspen, Colorado. For six years our research assistant, Bruce Taylor, operated a purchasing operation for a family-owned American jewelry manufacturer. Bruce lived in Bangkok, the principals lived in New York, the subcontractors were in Thailand and China, and the final manufacturing facilities where product was sent was in the Dominican Republic. These examples will be the norm, not the exception, in the Age of the Road Runner.

"Place" no longer matters—that is, you want to be in one place only when things outside are static, stable, slow-moving. But that's not the case anymore, so you want to be "placeless," or anyplace—anywhere you hang your laptop, modem, pager, cell phone—and yeah, hat—is "the office." The Road Runner spreads himself around everywhere. He's never in one place because . . . well, he's a road-RUNNER.

"What are you doing in your office?" asks the roadrunner leader incredulously. "Why aren't you working?" You can't be place-bound anymore. That's why the business model of credit card authorization king VeriFone is based on location independence, global reach, and electronic knowledge networks to "glue" everyone. Even giant companies like Mars, Nucor, Wal-Mart, and Virgin Atlantic have pitiful corporate headquarters. Ridiculously spare. The idea is not to get comfy in lush, opulent headquarters, but to get out on the road! In companies like Oticon and Chiat/Day, people don't even have offices anymore—your office is wherever you're hanging out today, with whomever you're working. In other words, the planet is the playground: We appear and operate with anyone, anywhere, and when we're far from each other we stay connected through e-mail and intranet, cell phone and fax, videoconferencing and overnight mail.

In contrast, coyotes plot tactics that require a stationary base—Wile E. perches atop a mountain, hides around a corner, or crouches behind a boulder. Most of his entrapment devices have him *lie* in *wait* for the *upright, stand-up, always-on-the-move* bird. We rarely see the Road Runner stand still for more than a fleeting moment. As Wile E. lies in wait, the Road Runner confidently speeds across the desert, averting his traps and tricks.

At Wal-Mart, Sam's Club managers are like the Road Runner. While preparing for a keynote address to senior management, Oren found it extremely hard to schedule a phone conversation with them. They were always *on the road*—visiting stores, customers, suppliers, technology experts, marketing specialists. Compare that with coyote organizations, where senior management is cloistered behind a wall of security and secretaries, and where their direct reports (taking their cue from their bosses) are comfortably ensconced behind big desks. If it takes a vote of toadies and public relations people for an outsider to reach an organization's CEO, you're probably dealing with a pack of coyotes!

The more "place" you have, the more baggage you carry . . . be it debt, sunk cost, bureaucratic infrastructure, passé product, rigid culture, or outdated tradition. One executive of a faltering Fortune 500 company ruefully told us, "Yeah, in our company we've got many years of tradition unmarred by progress." If the Road Runner were confined to a fixed place, the Coyote could easily catch him. For the Road Runner, "place of business" is anyplace he needs to be or simply where he is. Mobility is more important—the Road Runner can work anywhere, linked with whomever he needs to work, remotely or directly on site, and still be connected back "home."

No More Order

If order were the first order of business for the Road Runner, he would be road kill. His movements, no matter how fast, would be predictable. He wouldn't have a chance against the logic and reason of Wile E.'s schemes. The carefully developed blueprints, diagrams, and strategic plans Wile E. follows are all based on order and predictability: *Let's see . . . the Road Runner should come down this path at about this time. He will move from point A to point B, at which time I will ignite the engines of the Rocket Powered Roller Skates (guaranteed for quality and reliability). The wheels on the skates are perfectly angled to account for the precise forward path and speed of the prey . . . success is 101 percent assured.*

Typical coyote strategic planning! Today's premises logically extrapolated to generate complex scenarios that have everything in the future falling into place—perfectly. Thick documents called strategic plans, bulging manuals for policies and procedures, byzantine budgeting processes, intricate control and communication systems, complex interventions called TQM. Everything based on order—of time and place, of events, people, processes, and products. It's a once-marvelous system, created to make wars, manufacturing, and other acts of chaos manageable. But it is a system that works worse and worse every day.

Need proof? A Conference Board "State of Business" study concluded that the world of commerce today is marked by words like *turbulence, volatile environment,* and *unpredictable future.* Competitors' schemes, consumer preferences, technology and scientific advances, capital market shifts, demographic and social changes—they don't fall into place in the neat orderly way they used to. Even so, we spend precious time and resources propping up fat, slow bureaucracies dedicated to planning, TQM'ing, budgeting, reviewing, and signing off on documents—while the roadrunners around us bob and weave and skip merrily into new arenas with new concepts that make irrelevant, if not obsolete, what we are so earnestly doing today.

The leaders of two blue-chip American companies came to the same conclusion. In a *Wall Street Journal* interview, Doug Ivester, CEO of Coca-Cola, stated that within five years he hoped to do away with annual business plans altogether in favor of an ongoing, continuous planning process. The reason is twofold. First, there's simply no way for export-dependent Coke to predict, for example, an Asia crisis or the appearance of a new competitor. Second, traditional planning doesn't permit sufficiently quick response to changing conditions. Conventional planning processes only hopelessly bog down an organization's ability to respond to change. Andy Grove, the former Chairman of Intel, was even more blunt: "Think of your company as a fire department. It cannot predict where the next fire will take place, so it has to shape a flexible and efficient team that responds well to unanticipated events, no matter how extreme."

The skeptic might object: "I still have customers who expect quality products delivered on time. I still have shareholders that expect financial returns. I still have regulatory agencies that expect certain controls. I still have employees who expect to be paid." Of course you do! Everyone does.

But meeting those demands is simply the price of admission in today's business game. If that's all you do, you may survive in today's business desert, but you certainly won't thrive.

The Road Runner thrives because he zigs and zags, reading the requirements of the moment. Of course, he sniffs trends and does strategic thinking. He does this constantly, not once a year. In fact, he's much more attuned to the subtle shifts in the "desert market" than Wile E. He thrives in disorder. If his cartoon world were orderly and the Road Runner acted accordingly—even at warp speed—the Coyote, with his superior technology and cunning, would have him for breakfast. The reason the Road Runner frustrates Wile E. every time is that he is so unpredictable, so *dis-orderly.*

Wile E. thinks like a bureaucrat; the Road Runner thinks like an entrepreneur. The coyote relies on precision, precedent, and predictability—a linear, logical approach to achieving his goal. The Road Runner relies on ingenuity, imagination, and instinct—he takes a holistic, eclectic approach to living his life. The Road Runner knows that most order is concocted, controlling, and constrictive. He is a lover of freedom, riding the wind of a tornado that twists and turns, jumps and lands unpredictably across a landscape that itself is unpredictable and disorderly.

No More "Organization"

There will always be a need to organize people into focused activities. So, in that sense, "organizations" will continue to exist. The trouble is that our sense of what constitutes an organization is based largely on tried-and-true, but no longer operative, coyote thinking. We see organizations as:

- Buildings. Coyotes have edifice complexes. Roadrunners work out of their cars or on an airplane en route somewhere.
- Formal labels. Coyotes need titles ("Genius" on Wile E.'s business card). Coyotes like to know who are man-

agers and who are employees. Roadrunners see inside-outside logic as irrelevant and defy labeling. Is it a bird, an animated race car, or a wild comedian with weird colored feathers?

- Permanence. Coyotes love plans. They love structures, missions, and labor forces. They keep Acme forever. Roadrunners attach to nothing. They love results.

Instead, successful post–year 2000 organizations of two people or 200,000 are interlocked webs of alliances working anytime, anywhere to add new value. They are collaborative confederations of people with a common purpose: consolidating minds and energy to create something new. These alliances (often temporary) are confederations of equals, inside and outside—with permeability, and the ability to cross boundaries. A confederation means: "being united in an alliance." The connotation is: friend, companion, associate, accomplice, accessory, and ally.

A roadrunner employee could never survive (and would never find attractive) a coyote organization. As Tom Peters recently asked in his Web site in the wake of megamerger frenzy: "Why would any clever youngster with an iota of spunk want to go to work for one of the sluggish, bureaucratic, post-merger beasts???"

Why would any roadrunner want to work in any coyote organization, merged or otherwise? Roadrunners, for example, know that anyone talking about "empowering an employee" is most likely a coyote trying to masquerade as a roadrunner. Why? Because we've found an inverse relationship between the amount of leaders' big talk about empowerment (hot-air memos, splashy slogans) and the amount of empowerment that actually happens.

All too often, great pomp and ceremony about "pushing authority down" is followed by a slight slackening of controls here and a teeny bit of freedom to make a decision there. The coyote manager who benevolently grants a little more authority to "his people" (like he owns them) still gives them a subtle (or not-so-subtle) message, which goes something like this: "If you are planning on doing something interesting which is really different from standard operating procedure, make sure you first go through an exhausting, time-consuming clearance process . . . a process which will likely delay, dilute, or nix initiatives anyway."

And when it comes to relationships with other organizations, things become truly coyote-like. Acme is not a confederate (friend or ally) of the Coyote. The relationship is a mere business transaction . . . a formal, legalistic, commodity-like supplier-customer interface. You never see Acme reach out to Wile E. There is never a follow-up customer survey. Nobody at Acme says "We sell solutions, not products." Some faceless someone at Acme fills the order and mails it out. Caveat emptor. They don't even put a disclaimer on the box! Accordingly, the Road Runner simply uses brains and mobility to easily outmaneuver his foe:

There is a bowl filled with birdseed and a sign, "More Free Bird Seed," placed on the road. Directly above the bowl is a wooden beam straddling two cliffs. Wile E. is standing on one of the cliffs holding an anvil in his hands. The Road Runner runs up to the bowl and starts eating. Wile E. creeps along the beam, which breaks in half, sending him, the anvil, and the two pieces of beam falling. The Road Runner looks up and calmly takes one step to the left. Wile E. and the anvil plunge into the road, going all the way through. The broken pieces of beam land and cover up the hole. The Road Runner calmly steps onto the beams and resumes eating.

In coyote management, function follows form. As a consequence, managers frequently become protectors of processes, stewards of systems—they feed them, nurture them, protect them, identify with them. Function (like the goals and mission of the organization) takes a back seat. Coyote managers see control and precision as ends in themselves. Do that and you are professional; if you fail under those conditions, it must be unfair competition. As management consultant and *Stewardship* author Peter Block says: "If managers had to choose between uncontrolled excellence and highly controlled mediocrity, they would choose the latter." Coyote leaders focus on process and control. Roadrunners embrace any form necessary to achieve function.

No More Supremacy

Every Road Runner cartoon revolves around the same theme. We view events from the Coyote's perspective: He is obsessed with gaining supremacy over the bird—specifically, how to crush and devour it. The Road Runner has no interest in supremacy—over Wile E. or anyone else. His thinking is about roaring through the desert unencumbered. Applying the analogy to organizational life, roadrunner leaders think about excellence, accomplishment, achievement of extraordinary goals—and genuine power.

Power is about capability, competence, excellence, and the capacity to influence and inspire others to some grander way of doing things, whether you run a large consumer products division or a small procurement team. Powerful people do not need official rank and status for their power. Their "rule" is from a competence, an ethic, a philosophy, a value, a vision, a dedication to superb performance, an inspiring way of influencing. Governance happens by respecting a set of values rather than from bowing to rank.

Just as people sometimes confuse loyalty with allegiance, they confuse power with supremacy. Supremacy is about dominance, one-upmanship, beating someone, usurping authority, stealing status. It comes from the Latin word *supremus*, which means status—which by the way fits right into the linear world of coyote organizational hierarchy. The definition of *supremacy* is "highest in authority." Authority is about sovereignty and formally anointed rank, not about the ability to excel and to captivate others.

Supremacy, and its subset authority, are becoming irrelevant and counterproductive concepts in the roadrunner world. They're unrealistic. Nowadays, it is becoming increasingly difficult for any company, even a successful one, to gain and maintain a supreme position. For example, the biggest, strongest players in prescription pharmaceuticals, the Mercks and Glaxo Wellcomes of the world, each own only a 5 to 7 percent global market share. In the highly lucrative personal banking sector, Citibank is a big player with $1 billion in revenues; yet its share of the world market is less than 1 percent (put the top ten banks together in this niche and you've got a grand total of about 6 percent share). Starbucks and Dell Computer, both extraordinary success stories in the 1990s, have less than 10 percent of their respective markets.

New competitors challenge big, entrenched, presumably "supreme" players every day. Kodak's woes are aggravated by the challenges of Hewlett-Packard and Casio divvying up the digital imaging photography market. Travel agents and car dealers are under assault by the rapid development of online search-and-buy capabilities. Tiny upstarts like N2K, Liquid Audio, SuperSonicBoom, Headspace, EMusic, CDNow, and CDUctive challenge the global giants who manufacture and distribute compact disks—offering online sales, purchasing, and logistics, plus click-of-the-mouse customized CDs. While it's hard for outsiders to believe, Intel has been successful because its operating credo is "only the paranoid survive," and Microsoft echoes this belief by literally operating as if it has two years left in business.

Free markets free roadrunners. In the 1970s, Sears and

IBM were acknowledged as supreme by everyone, including themselves; both almost collapsed in the face of roadrunner competitors. It took new CEOs Arthur Martinez and Lou Gerstner, who stripped arrogance and a sense of invincibility from the ranks, for both companies to perform surprising turnarounds. A dozen years ago, Apple Computer had the sweetest margins and the coolest brand name in personal computers; a dozen years ago McDonald's was rated by one analyst as "a perpetual growth machine." Things change. Supremacy is a false idol. Many once-supreme companies no longer exist. Apple and Sears are coming back from near-death experiences. As Arthur Martinez reminds his troops: "Today's peacock is tomorrow's feather duster."

Once upon a time, when coyotes ruled, "survival of the fittest" meant that the largest, most massive organizations prospered. Wile E. Coyote dwarfs the Road Runner—he's bigger, stockier, and has all that technology from Acme. He *should* kick tail. Why doesn't he? Because the Road Runner uses his talents, ingenuity, wit, "street smarts," imagination, and humor. He always laughs at the Coyote before the closing credits. Wile E. Coyote may think he has supremacy, but the Road Runner has the real power.

In the twenty-first century, roadrunners will rule! The trademarks of roadrunner organizations are anytime-any-place-anything thinking and work driven by purpose. Roadrunners are sharply focused—but not on a predictable solution or "outcome," like MBO or meeting the budget or strategic plan. They are focused on purpose—not on "avoiding failure" or "avoiding coyote" (that is just a necessary tactic in the marketplace), but on the pursuit of joy and excellence, consistent with who they are and what their competencies are. In that framework, the sky's the limit, and the coyote (aka the competition) is an insignificant, amusing blip.

Wile E. Coyote: aka: Evereadii Eatibus, Carnivorous Vulgaris, Eatius Birdius, Famishius Famishius, Eatius-Slobbius, Famishius Fantasticus, Eternalii Famishiis

Last Books Read: *Western Cookery, The Art of Road Runner Trapping*

Favorite Movie: *The Birds*

Favorite Bedtime Story: "Chicken Little"

Favorite Hero In History: Machiavelli

Occupation: Aerialist Extraordinaire, Explosive Expert, Mechanical and Aeronautical Engineer, Self-Proclaimed "Genius"

Primary Threat: Gravity

If He Had a Party He'd Invite: James Audubon, Calvin Coolidge, Rambo

Hobbies: Explosives, skydiving, reading Acme Manufacturing catalogs

Best Line: "He's mine . . . just mine . . . and I'm gonna die trying"

The Road Runner: aka : Digoutius-hot-rodis, Accelerati Incredibilus, Delicius-Delicius, Burnius Roadius, Digoutius-Unbelievable, Dig-Outius Tid-Bitius, Tastius Supersonicus, Birdibus Zippibus

Last Book Read: Claims to be illiterate (but we know he's kidding!)

Favorite Movie: *Dances with Wolves*

Favorite Bedtime Story: "Little Red Riding Hood"

Favorite Hero in History: St. Francis of Assisi

Occupation: Part-time Owner, Road Runner Manufacturing Company, a global network of catapult makers

Primary Threat: None he can't handle

If He Had a Party He'd Invite: Ted Turner, Leonardo da Vinci, Groucho Marx, Howard Stern

Hobbies: Coyote watching

Best Line: "Beep Beep!"

CHAPTER 3

A Road Runner, Not a Road Warrior: A Map for Leaders

In the *Road Warrior* movies, Mel Gibson operated in a post-apocalyptic future where brawn, fast vehicles, and a stockpile of gasoline were the tools of success. There were no rules: It was anything goes in a violently primitive world. Many businesspeople today fancy themselves as "road warriors," though they wouldn't last five seconds in Gibson's world.

The business world today operates within a certain set of rules, explicit and implicit, which makes it the antithesis of the Gibson world: hierarchy, command and control, legalistic emphasis in dealings with insiders and outsiders, uniformity in processes, standardization and scale, formality in systems and policies, unity of command, order, line of authority, division of work, job descriptions, functionalism, authority matched to responsibility, rational decision-making, contractual relationship with outsiders, adherence to rules and processes. While different organizations deviate from one rule or another in varying degrees, there is an implicit acceptance of their validity overall in managing an enterprise. Indeed, these rules reflect what we often call "professional management."

Yet the rules themselves are not sacrosanct. They were developed by social analysts like Max Weber and Henri Fayol in the late 1800s and early 1900s and refined by individuals like General Motors Chairman Alfred Sloan and academic Robert Merton. Once appropriate in light of the huge shifts in work and business engendered by the Industrial Revolution from the mid-1800s through the latter part of the twentieth century, those rules have decreasing validity, and an increasing number of organizations are finding that rigidly following them may mean competitive disaster.

But what's the alternative? In the Age of the Road Runner, business success will come by adhering to a new set of rules, and those leaders who *start now* to adopt these rules will position their organizations—and careers—for competitive advantage in the twenty-first century. Let's look at one such leader.

A Road Runner in Chicago

Oren first met Glen Tullman in 1993, while doing research for his book *Jumping the Curve: Innovation and Strategic Choice in an Age of Transition.* At the time, Glen was the president and COO of CCC Information Services, a Chicago-based company he founded with his brother and two other individuals in 1982. What impressed Oren was that this $90 million company had not only been enjoying a 40 percent annual growth rate, but had gone head-to-head with companies ten times its size and beaten them by being faster and smarter— specifically by revolutionizing three lines of business in the unsexy auto collision estimating business. How'd they do that?

First, CCC *reinvented* the total loss valuation market. Traditionally, insurance companies (CCC's customers) used "blue" or "red" books (produced by large, powerful vendors) to appraise the full value of cars that were lost, stolen, or damaged beyond repair. These appraisal books were published every three to four months and distributed nationally, which meant that the data was seldom current and it never reflected regional variations in value. To remedy these complaints, CCC developed the largest computerized used car database in the world based on "real steel," vehicles actually inventoried on thousands of new and used car lots across the country. Their system not only included regionalized data on car values but broke it down by mileage, style, features, options, and price. Plus, the database was updated continuously. Small wonder that insurers found that using CCC's database not only saved their adjusters significant time but also provided appraisals that were more acceptable to both their policyholders and regulators. Eleven years later, CCC had collared 90 percent of the computerized total loss evaluation market.

Next, CCC went head-to-head with a couple of billion-dollar competitors in the much larger collision estimating market. The industry norm was a process adjuster's spec sheets using mainframe computers. Anyone needing the information waited . . . and waited. There were errors galore. CCC did away with all that paper flow by developing EZEst, a collision estimating software product. EZEst allowed the adjuster to write an estimate out in the field, right at the car, on a laptop computer. Once again, insurance companies marveled at the real-time speed and increased accuracy of the appraisal data, which translated into a 30 percent cost reduction in the estimating process. The results for CCC? In the first eighteen months of entering the business, CCC's market share went from zero to 30 percent and today stands in excess of 60 percent.

CCC's third undertaking was its most audacious: to reinvent the entire collision insurance supply chain. Traditionally, a policyholder had to obtain several estimates before the typical insurer would authorize repair work. So, garages would inflate their estimates and the insurance companies would beat them down. Eventually, the two distrustful adversaries would reach a compromise, and the exhausted, irritated customer would finally get the work done on the car.

What CCC did was build an electronic network, called

EZnet, to connect insurers directly to carefully selected repair facilities. The policyholder could choose among different participating vehicle repair shops. The new business model turned the selected repair shops into partners with the insurers and replaced the rancor in their former relationships with trust and honesty. Body shops and insurers were using the same system. By the time the policyholder dropped off the vehicle at the garage, EZnet had already transmitted the policy information to the garage, arranged for the rental car to be waiting, and ordered parts for the car's repair.

"With EZnet, we're now selling a better process through our network, not just an estimate," said Tullman back in 1994, likening the whole business model to an "HMO for cars." By compressing the entire cycle from fourteen days to seven days, both the policyholders and insurers were more than satisfied—which helps explain why CCC today includes over 15,000 collision repair shops and 350 insurance companies across the country into its new network. Today, the company dominates the collision estimating market with over $150 million in revenues—and yesterday's big players, the billion-dollar behemoths, are no longer leaders, but followers.

A Roadrunner Reappears

In 1995, a year and a half after he wrote about CCC in *Jumping the Curve,* Oren heard from Glen Tullman again. Glen called to say that he had left CCC a few months earlier to take the CEO position at Enterprise Systems. Located near Chicago, the new company was a health care information service provider that developed software and services that allowed large health care organizations to reduce their operational costs dramatically, especially in the areas of materials and facilities management, scheduling and logistics, and financial systems like general ledger and accounts payable.

Tullman took over for a CEO and founder who created

some great individual products but was at risk of being integrated out of business by the big players, billion-dollar companies like HBOC and SMS.

At the time Tullman commented, "Being best of breed isn't enough. We need a broader vision for where we are taking our company and our customers." Tullman created a new category called resource management that combined materials management, scheduling and logistics, and financial systems—the right resource at the right time at the right cost.

As with CCC, Tullman's approach was to capitalize on information technology to change an entire business process, in this case how the nonclinical health care operations were managed. The process started with scheduling a patient. That event triggered "resource calls," electronic scheduling of physicians, nurses, reservations for operating rooms, and automated materials ordering. The result: better health care delivered at a lower cost. And, for the first time, health care organizations started to understand their costs, which allowed them to improve.

Then, in early 1998, Glen Tullman called again! Enterprise had been so successful that it had been wooed and bought out a few months earlier by one of the big players, HBOC, for $250 million. Glen had been invited to take a senior corporate position in the acquiring firm but declined because he was more intrigued with an offer from yet another Chicago-based company to be its CEO.

Glen's new company, Allscripts, based near Chicago in Libertyville, Illinois, has a singular mission: to change the way America receives its medications. Allscripts provides point-of-care medication management and distribution software that allows physicians to write prescriptions electronically and either send them to pharmacies or in most cases dispense medications directly to patients at the point-of-care, right in the doctor's office—bypassing the visit to the pharmacy altogether and fixing a process most people are unhappy with today—waiting in line at a pharmacy. The result—a faster, more convenient, confidential, and accurate process that costs less and results in more people actually taking their medications.

Let's set the stage. Almost three billion times a year a physician scrawls illegible handwriting on a prescription pad, patients take the "script" to a pharmacy, and millions of times a year, the pharmacy calls back to suggest alternatives based on managed care recommendations. Time-consuming, expensive, and not patient focused. The new process is road-runner revolutionary.

It works like this. A physician, using Allscripts' TouchScript software, electronically writes a script with three touches of her finger and in less than twenty seconds. As fast as a hand-written script. But, because the software has verified the opportunity, managed care formularies, and checked the script for drug interactions, pharmacy callbacks are dramatically reduced. At this point, the physician is notified if the medication prescribed is in stock. If so, she scans a bar code on the bottle and hands the patient a prepackaged medication. One-stop, patient-focused health care.

That simple bar code scan just like a grocery store not only completes safety checks, but triggers a just-in-time ordering and production system that dials up Allscripts' computers each night and replenishes drugs as needed. The learning-based software can predict 80 percent of the medications that will be prescribed (the remaining 20 percent are sent electronically to a local pharmacy). To make it easier, Allscripts' software now runs on standard PCs, touch screens, and hand-held devices like the PalmPilot, which easily fit into a physician's pocket.

Prior to Glen's arrival, Allscripts had grown to be a $25 million company. He foresees Allscripts' sales to exceed $100 million this year and add a whole new distribution channel to the pharmacy industry, which exceeds $100 billion in expenditures each year. Glen says that "patients will soon expect physicians to provide medications as a normal course of business just as they expect banks to have cash stations. It's all about convenience and choice. As health care becomes a business, patients will no longer be patient."

Rara Avis

If we could put Glen Tullman in a roadrunner costume in the cartoon series, against his bigger coyote competitors, he'd feel right at home. He truly is a rara avis, a rare bird. He exhibits at least five of the key personal characteristics that distinguish roadrunner leaders from coyote leaders.

Coyotes Are Earnest; Roadrunners Are Passionate

The Road Runner has a passionate and confident look... like a rare bird enjoying its work. Wile E. is serious and earnest. He views his challenge with solemn gravity. Coyotes work from a sense of duty or obligation; roadrunners are fueled by spirit and joy. Coyotes are compulsive; roadrunners committed.

Time and again we watch Wile E. paint a tunnel on the side of the mountain hoping to lure the Road Runner into smashing into it. When the Road Runner races right through the illusory tunnel, Wile E. is stunned. "I must have created a magic tunnel with my paint!" he marvels. So he attempts to enter his own picture . . . and reality flattens his face as well as his spirit.

We may laugh, but we also sympathize with the Coyote. If only he could believe in "TV magic," as children often label the unexplainable on television, maybe he could defy the laws of physics like the Road Runner. It's a lesson for us all. The roadrunner organizations of tomorrow must take repeated leaps of faith to break the restraints of rationality in search of a more creative outcome. The spirited associates who inhabit them must view obstacles as opportunities and barriers as bequests. This is the perfect description of Glen Tullman.

Roadrunners like Glen do not take "hops of faith" or "jumps of faith." They take passionate leaps. *Leap* implies lunging or soaring beyond what is required to make it to the other side. There is a "throw caution to the wind" air about them. *Hops* suggest timidity. Jumps are calculated to be adequate or sufficient. The Road Runner's leap of faith is unbridled. Roadrunners do not measure their faith by the spoonful, but by the handfuls! They TRUST, or they don't. However, their faith is not a blind trust, but rather one grounded in close-to-the-customer market awareness and passionate commitment.

"To succeed," says Scott Cook, CEO of Intuit, "you need people who have a whole bunch of passion, and you can't just order someone to be passionate about a business direction." Passion comes from a deep sense of purpose, not the "ought to" sense of purpose that drives "civic duty," for example, or a "need to mow the lawn" obligation. The roadrunner passion is the "can't wait to" enthusiasm of an employee on fire. As Milacron's EVP Alan Shaffer said at their winter 1998 corporate retreat: "Our goal is not merely to get buy-in. I want to put a lump in their throats and a tear in their eyes. I want to take their breath away."

Passionate employees are oblivious to the time clocks. Passion-filled employees practice generosity thinking, or what Stephen Covey labeled an "abundance mentality" (rather than a "scarcity mentality"). They are so inspired by their purpose and mission that they give without thought of 50-50 balance or quid pro quo reciprocity.

Passion drives a Glen Tullman company. Roadrunner-like leaders such as Glen don't seem to waste energy worrying about coming up short tomorrow or fretting over what might have been yesterday. Yet his business philosophy has an unexpected, unconventional but important tenet: Have fun. "You gotta have fun. You gotta be doing something that you

43

love and enjoy," Glen says. Then you don't look at the clock. Then you're really committed. Then you have faith and confidence to pursue what's never been done. Then you accomplish what the current industry powerhouses (the coyotes) say can't be done. "If that doesn't exist," says Tullman, "all the money in the world won't make the difference."

Magic is another word that crops up in the Glen Tullman lexicon, more than words like *scale* and *synergy*. "When steps, goals, and processes seem to blend to the point of disappearance, it's like magic," he marvels. "We want to make the patient problem disappear, like magic, using technology to design a better process." It's as magical as the roadrunner disappearing into the mountain "tunnel," leaving the earnest, diligent Wile E. baffled. Writer Arthur C. Clarke says, "Any sufficiently advanced technology is indistinguishable from magic."

Faith, fun, passion, magic. No wonder the earnest coyotes of the business world are perpetually frustrated . . . and constantly hungry!

Coyotes Follow Procedure; Roadrunners Experiment

Coyotes methodically follow the standard operating procedure; they dutifully adhere to the rules of the organization and industry—this is how we play the game. Wile E. consistently follows the Acme blueprint to the letter. While the latest "catch a bird" contraption is always accurately constructed, it is never effective. The sideline coach in us all wants to tell him to trust his instincts instead of Acme's instructions. We wish he would step back and look at what's going on around him rather than staying focused on what's right in front of his nose.

Roadrunners know the procedures all right, but whenever necessary they have a healthy disrespect for them—and are more than willing to make exceptions and take risks in order to boost performance and innovation. The quest for a more elegant result or more novel solution propels roadrunners to be ever-inventive roadrunners going outside the proverbial nine dots. They craft new solutions to old challenges. Simply put, they try stuff . . . stuff that often violates conventional wisdom. When Glen Tullman ran CCC, he wasn't interested in producing a "continuously improved" blue book, nor was he interested in producing a cost-efficient spec-sheet-to-mainframe process. Instead, he concentrated on experiments and goals that would reinvent the industry. As leadership consultant Gary Heil says, "Edison did not start out to improve the candle."

Glen Tullman remains personally committed to creating experimental organizations. "What's exciting for me is re-thinking and redesigning and reinventing—creating a different way and a better way of doing something. You don't need to be a CEO to do that. But as a leader, that's the organization spirit I try to create, because I want those kinds of people working with me. Yes, I run the organization with a minimum of structure and hierarchy, but the reason is because I want to encourage fast, aggressive experimentation."

Glen Tullman is clear about his role. He wants to create an environment that attracts, retains, and develops a certain kind of people: roadrunner people who want to understand the whole game, the whole company, the whole business—not just their "job"; people who think like businesspeople and owners—not like narrowly focused employees who follow rules and crave order. "Everyone is a contributor," Glen says. "We want everyone to feel a sense of responsibility to take *whatever initiative is necessary* to help us succeed in our cause. . . . I look for people who can tell me how they would run our business, or any business, better."

Enterprise Systems, for example, brought all hands into the business by spreading information everywhere; in its paperless, fully electronic environment, any employee could access any information immediately—be it financial data, marketing data, competitive data, whatever. Second, the culture was such that everyone was expected to challenge the process continually in pursuit of organizational goals so large and dramatic that they seemed impossible. Third, the environment was such that any employee could go (in fact, was expected to go) anywhere electronically or physically to join forces with anyone to make decisions fast and get stuff done. The whole idea was: Do something, try something, and fast! If you make mistakes, fine; learn from them; share your learning from them.

Glen's view on failure is pure roadrunner: Encourage more on-purpose failures. This means that you expect people to make mistakes . . . but they will be errors in sync with mission or vision. An "error" might be a mistake in going too far to delight a customer or it might involve using too many resources or too much time to develop a new process or product. Failures made in pursuit of a vision are labors to be lauded, not bummers to be blamed. Trust comes from experience; experience from risks. The only route to courageous actions and experimental efforts begins with on-purpose failure.

Roadrunner leaders like Glen also encourage associates to understand the whole game—to be businesspeople, not just followers of rules and procedure. The more they think like owners, the more they will be willing to explore, experiment, and expand to solution thinking ("How can we . . .") rather than barrier bitching ("We can't because . . ."). Additionally, they will begin to act more like people who need a leader who partners rather than one who parents.

"It all comes down to this," says Glen: "If you don't make dust, you eat dust. You have to have people who aren't afraid to take risks, to explore new ideas and new environments. In so many companies, you've got a bunch of aggressive people working hard, but they're going in the wrong direction because they're aggressive and hardworking in the same old way. You've got to look at things and try things in a new way." Nowadays, it's riskier not to take the risks to break the pattern.

Coyotes Are Resilient;
Roadrunners Are Resourceful

There is a side to Wile E.'s dogged determination that most of us find admirable. That is . . . until the next cartoon when he uses the same old tactic to the same bad end. He is locked into a cycle of "get a scheme—set a trap—get snookered—get smashed." The resourceful Road Runner slips away unscathed, leaving behind a cloud of dust and a glimpse of his triumphant countenance. "Beep Beep" resonates across the New Mexico desert.

How do you create a resourceful workforce? By creating an environment that is resource-full—full of resources. For Glen, it starts with state-of-the-art technology. Training and development is another vital resource in Glen's arsenal—we'll talk about that shortly. But there's another factor. Glen has learned that it's collaboration that really drives up resourcefulness. *Collaboration* literally means "co-labor." Working together. Looking at the challenges and opportunities together. Accessing whatever information we need—together. Feeling a sense of urgency and excitement—together. Taking bold action—together. Knowing we can be frank with each other, trust each other, and count on each other—together. Collaborators are the kind of people Tullman hires and promotes at all levels, in all functions. That's the kind of environment he tries to cultivate, for he knows that when people experience that kind of support and safety—from each other and from the leader—they feel free to respond with ingenuity and imagination—together. Resourceful leads to resource-full. "It's about the fun of the chase—together," he says.

When you talk to Glen Tullman you'll never hear the words *my people* or *those people* or *people who work for me*. Instead, you'll hear about "the people I work with" or "our team." "Us," not "me." One story Glen was proudest of was when a customer told him, "I don't know which of you people runs this place." When people hold hands and jump into the fun of the chase, resourcefulness emerges.

Coyotes Are Shrewd;
Roadrunners Are Wise

Tomorrow's winners will rely on the irrational as well as the rational. Fables will be as honored as facts; figures will keep company with visions. Creative solutions will be grounded in gut as well as logic.

Wile E.'s shrewdness is grounded in a linear logic. He carefully studies the blueprint of his latest "catch the bird" gizmo from Acme and concludes, "If the bird comes through this valley and I have a big stone on the edge supported by a tiny rock tied to a string stretched across the ledge of the mountain down to the lookout spot around the bend in the road . . ." Invariably his step-by-step method fails. Armed with wisdom, the Road Runner ends up intuiting an alternate approach, a radical new escape theory.

The 1990s will be remembered as the beginning of the era of the learning organization. Wise companies now focus on facilitating learning, not only to create storehouses and electronic depositories of information, but also to encourage the pursuit of inquiry, insight, and intuition. They see learning as a tool for adaptation and responsiveness, as a mental discipline that helps the organization remain on the cutting edge.

How do you encourage and nurture wisdom? First, you hire and promote people with talent, not skills. Skills become obsolete fast. Skills keep us in a comfortable rut. Remember that "fun" was a major tenet of Glen's business philosophy? Here's another: "Make sure you're learning. Otherwise, you're going downhill, because someone else is learning."

"Demand learning," Glen says. "Don't wait for the organization to offer it. Read widely. Think extensively, not just about your job, but about the company, the industry, the planet, life. Join teams; join networks; volunteer to take on tasks and projects you never have done in the past. Try new experiences. Create new experiences. Sometimes the people I want to promote aren't ready because they haven't taken the initiative to create the experiences for themselves."

Glen believes his job as CEO is to create an environment where everyone views learning as strategically vital and personally attractive. It boils down to this:

- Hire razor-sharp, curious, obstreperous people (those who ask, inquire, probe, investigate, try things out, challenge). Provide them with a constant supply of training and education opportunities in order to fan their flames.
- Expect everyone to initiate and demand learning, to grow their own expertise, and to share it with others (face-to-face, newsletters, intranet) so that the whole organization grows in its expertise.
- Seek people who agree on values and priorities, but who think differently about how to get there. Avoid people who think exactly alike. Encourage people to teach each other—in cross-disciplinary projects, in meetings, in bars.
- Seek people who seek varied experiences. Not just work experiences, but life experiences. A sales manager at Enterprise left to bum around the world. He launched a small bungee-jumping business in Indonesia. When he came back, Glen hired him on the spot to direct sales efforts at Allscripts. Why? He had demonstrated initiative and curiosity, and he had created an experience from which he learned a lot.
- Encourage people to read and think—and not just trade publications. Glen Tullman reads two books and fifty to seventy publications a month—from *Forbes* and *Mother Jones* to *Tokyo Today*. He does this to expand his field of vision constantly, his radarscope of opportuni-

ties, his awareness of critical trends, his inspiration and courage to proceed.

Roadrunner leaders become mentors; boss parenting is replaced with leader partnering. "I get a tremendous pleasure in teaching and mentoring," says Tullman, "and in seeing people win." Good leaders are voyeurs; they get excited seeing others' successes. The real excitement in business is watching people grow, realize their dreams, make their lives better. "You build a successful company by building successful people."

Just as the Road Runner constantly observes and learns in the cartoons, leaders also know that learning is never over. As the world continues to get more complex, roadrunner leaders know they must always be helping others stay busy at learning. Active learners more easily and more effectively deal with change. Just as machines need proper maintenance to go the distance, so do people.

Coyotes Look Back; Roadrunners Look Ahead

Watch a number of Road Runner cartoons. You will begin to notice that for every time the Road Runner looks back, Wile E. looks back many times. The spirit of the Road Runner is about pathbreaking progress, not hidebound tradition. Coyotes say "It won't work" or "We tried that back in the winter of '74." Roadrunners say "Why not?" and "Let's invent some new rules." Roadrunners know that it's best to use history and tradition as a spotlight to the future, not as anchor to the past. Roadrunners say: "Don't look back because we're not going in that direction."

Put together all the pieces of roadrunner vs. coyote described thus far, and you can summarize Glen's management philosophy: Fan the flames of speed, innovation, ingenuity, initiative, world-class talent, cutting-edge expertise, and perpetual development—all aimed at looking forward—that is, all aimed at achieving gargantuan missions and audacious goals that serve to lead and create markets, not merely "respond" to them. That's what has fueled CCC, Enterprise, and Allscripts. This is how a roadrunner leader creates a roadrunner organization.

In summary, roadrunners are as different in spirit from coyotes as flamboyant entrepreneurs are from stodgy bureaucrats. Becoming a roadrunner requires transformation not imitation; metamorphosis not mimicry. Read the pathetic sidebar from the Darwin Society about the fate of one wannabe!

 The Darwin Award Goes to a Wannabe Wile E.

The Darwin Award is sponsored by Blue Ribbon Skyhawk and given annually to the "person or persons who did the world gene pool a big service by exterminating themselves in the most extraordinarily stupid way—before reproducing in kind." This 1996 winner of the award tragically reminds us that brains are more crucial than bravado, and the real thing is more important than blind imitation. Like Wile E., we admire a "never say die" relentlessness. However, when the race is over, it is the roadrunner manner that emerges victorious.

The Arizona Highway Patrol came upon a pile of smoldering metal embedded into the side of a cliff rising above the apex of a curve. The wreckage resembled the site of an airplane crash, but it was a car. The type of car was unidentifiable at the scene. The police lab finally figured out what it was and what had happened.

It seems a guy had somehow gotten hold of a JATO unit (Jet Assisted Take Off—actually a solid-fuel rocket) that is used to give heavy military transport planes an extra "push" for taking off from short airfields. He had driven his Chevy Impala out into the desert and found a long, straight stretch of road. Then, he attached the JATO to his car, jumped in, got up some speed, and fired off the JATO!

The facts (as best could be determined) are that the operator of the 1967 Chevrolet Impala hit JATO ignition at a distance of approximately 4.0 miles from the crash site. This was established by the prominent scorched and melted asphalt at that location. The JATO, if operating properly, would have reached maximum thrust within 5 seconds, causing the Chevy to reach speeds well in excess of 350 mph and continuing at full power for approximately 20–25 seconds.

The driver (soon-to-be-pilot) most likely would have experienced G-forces usually reserved for dog-fighting F-14 jocks under full afterburners, basically causing him to become insignificant for the remainder of the event. However, the automobile remained on the straight highway for about 2.5 miles (15–20 seconds) before the driver applied and completely melted the brakes, blowing the tires and leaving thick rubber marks on the road surface. The car then became airborne for an additional 1.4 miles, impacting the cliff face at a height of 125 feet and leaving a crater 3 feet deep in the rock.

Most of the driver's remains were not recoverable; however small fragments of bone, teeth and hair were extracted from the crater and fingernail and bone shards were removed from a piece of debris believed to be a portion of the Impala's steering wheel.

The New Rules of the Road

The Age of the Road Runner comes with new rules of the road. Just as road warrior Mel Gibson succeeded by mastering a new world, success in the future business world will require observing completely new rules. Over the next seven chapters, we will explore each rule in depth and show how people with the attributes of the Road Runner are those that will best adapt to—and be aligned with—those rules.

Some have stated that the new rules of the road are simply the rules of the Internet. The new terrain of business value will not be conducted solely in the uncharted intangible domain of cyberspace. Today's stampede into the wild, woolly (intangible) terrain of cyberspace is like the situation in the 1800s when gold rushers galloped into the unknown (tangible) areas of California and Alaska in search of gold. Today's corporate gold rushers search for IPOs and e-commerce opportunities, but the principle is the same.

The world today is similar to the challenge 500 years ago when folks like Sir Francis Drake, Vasco da Gama, and Christopher Columbus set forth into the (tangible) unknowns with the same foresight and courage that today's pathfinders are doing in the (intangible) unknowns. But remember: Drake et al.'s maps and premises were based on the realities of the time, and hence were 90 percent wrong in their assumptions and predictions. Nevertheless, Drake and his colleagues plunged into the void and carved out a new era. The analogy remains the same today, though again, much of it is intangible, much of it is in a fourth-dimensional space.

But remember that the Internet metaphor, no matter how sexy and exciting, isn't complete enough. Whether you are established or start-up there's still heaps of crucial tangibles in balance sheets and interpersonal relations (real people, real products, real hardware, real offices) that any business leader has to deal with. And even when it comes to the Web, e-commerce, and the like, leaders of enterprises still need some practical rules to navigate these new waters.

In other words, the Age of the Road Runner will operate in both tangible space *and* cyberspace. What's crucial is two things. First, the Age of the Road Runner will make entirely new demands of those who wish to race in it, just like the age of Drake, da Gama, and Columbus made entirely new demands on them. Second, because of this, the Age of the Road Runner will demand new rules of play for those who wish to be serious contenders. To prepare for the race, then, here's a quick word collage overview of the rules that will define the Age of the Road Runner.

Rule 1: Everyone Is a Full Player

Universal membership . . . everyone can be more like the Road Runner . . . egalitarian culture . . . open-book management . . . every employee an owner . . . You, Inc. . . . demise of rank and emergence of a brain-based economy . . . no more secrets . . . employees who go through tunnels painted on the side of mountains . . . full player means fully engaged . . . everybody plans . . . no benchwarmers. Make 100 percent inclusion your modus operandi.

Rule 2: All Boundaries Are Permeable

If boundaries are permeable, then why not have as few as possible? . . . information, resources, and people flow freely . . . roadrunners are herd-proof . . . maniacs with a mission . . . organizations are domesticators . . . boundaries are not real . . . think in wholes, inclusion, webs, multi-everything . . . freedom is what you have left when arrogance, aimlessness, ignorance, and fear are removed . . . power flows better through direct connections. Cultivate tight connections around the world.

Rule 3: All Enterprise Is Virtual

Nothing lasts . . . fashion . . . all products are experiments . . .
perpetual reinvention . . . everything you do will be virtual,
including how you learn, who you work with, who you learn
with . . . creating your own destiny and security . . . organizations that work in the virtual mode love the desert . . . let go
of everything but your world-class talent and your soul. Stay
light and unencumbered.

Rule 4: Honorable Cultures Are Powerful

Promote values that attract people with impeccable
honor . . . free yourself from rules that bind and imprison . . .
put ethics, trust, openness in communication . . . value and
dignity of each individual . . . spirituality of the culture . . .
Ritz-Carlton . . . Southwest Airlines . . . Harley-Davidson . . .
ESPN . . . E*Trade . . . Yahoo! . . . importance of character
and courage . . . Road Runner's joy vs. Wile E.'s grim pursuit . . . effortlessness of a character-based work world . . . no
baggage to carry. Keep honor—lose drag.

Rule 5: Mastery Is the Magic

Masterful organizations have strong authority in the marketplace . . . perpetual learning, networking . . . relevant competence rises to the levels of mastery . . . mastery is individual
and collective . . . roadrunners are masters of magical speed
and agility . . . Wile E. repeats his errors endlessly . . . mastery
is always unfinished . . . the confidence makers . . . fostering
the spirit of inquiry . . . creating a curious organization. Become the fastest learner in your industry.

Rule 6: Breakthrough Is the Road to Prosperity

Roadrunners are first, exceptional, unique . . . break rules, ignore conventional wisdom, create markets . . . differentiation in a crowded marketplace . . . constantly raising the bar . . . institutionalized courage . . . second place doesn't last . . . neither do breakthroughs . . . the rebellious confederation vs. the composed organization . . . the door to success, not the key . . . innovation plus implementation . . . swimming upstream. Go in a different direction than everyone else.

Rule 7: The Last Word Is . . . Laughter

Wile E. and Road Runner are meant to make us laugh . . . the power of joy in survival and success . . . laughter separates us from animals . . . organizational giggling as a strategic priority . . . fostering gaiety is not silliness . . . Warren Buffett . . . authenticity and success . . . laughter leading to productivity, imagination, innovation, attracting and retaining the top talent . . . Herb Kelleher . . . without joy, there is no soul . . . without soul, there is no inspiration. Throw out joy to your customers and employees. *Fun* shall be the last word.

Tail Feathers: A Roadrunner on Fire

Some roadrunners are intense and serious; some are intense and . . . fun. Bridget Bilinski is one of the latter. Vice President of Franchising for Courtyard by Marriott, she has been known since high school as someone with a quick wit who could make anything funny. After joining Marriott in 1979, she quickly moved up the ranks by establishing a reputation as a fun-loving cheerleader.

> Having fun and working hard has always been a critical element to my work life. I think I stood out because I wanted to do my job, my way. . . . In fact, the only time I've ever been disciplined as a manager was due to being *too* happy. As a desk manager at a large airport hotel, we quite often had to work "killer Fridays." We would check out 800 people in three hours and check in another 400—VERY BUSY, lots of lines, and lots of edgy guests. I always felt my role was to entertain the room, and I'd get other staff to join with me. Quite often the guests would jump into our playfulness and join the show too. My boss thought that our behavior was not professional and wrote me up. It had never occurred to me that you couldn't look at practically everything with a sense of joy.

Roadrunner leadership according to Bridget not only means laughing—every day; it also means knowing how to promote energetic, collaborative work groups. "I not only want people who work with me to laugh," she says, "but to use laughter to create great synergy and a contagious passion. This creates the kind of team other groups and stakeholders enjoy working with. The goal is to have people or groups bouncing ideas off each other, looking for win-wins, and recommending solutions! Roadrunners create constant interplay between groups."

There's more to roadrunner teamwork than lots of laughter and creative synergy, though. There are three ways to spot a team of roadrunners, according to Bridget: "First, people on a roadrunner team know a lot about themselves and each other. This is more than work—it is family! If we're going to be effective we need to understand each other's histories, strengths, preferences, and values.

"Second, a roadrunner team has a vision of greatness. I believe that teams become passionate and cohesive when they're striving for something that's truly great—truly epic! This means striving for results that seem impossible, yet, when accomplished, give the team a sense of being a part of something unbelievable and historic.

"Third, roadrunner teams celebrate. Not traditional-empty-stuffy-nonpersonal kind of celebration but emotionally honest and meaningful acclaim. In my world, if someone is going to be praised, it had better bring big laughs or big tears. This is the kind of recognition that motivates people to work to their optimum level and be the best they can be."

One of her examples of a "truly epic" achievement was her experience as the new general manager of a Marriott hotel in Arizona.

> I went into a broken situation, with the lowest Associate Opinion Survey (AOS) scores in the region and profit margins slipping year to year.
>
> We immediately did team building throughout the entire hotel (130 associates) and set stretch goals that were unheard of. All associates were trained on the financial situation of the property and how their roles impacted the bottom line. We did similar training on guest satisfaction. We introduced new tools to track their progress. All of a sudden, the entire staff was beginning to think like owners. Light bulbs started going off and performance began to shift.
>
> We created new opportunities for sharing ideas and information across all areas. Cross-training between departments was the next natural step, and people began to teach each other. Defenses came down and what blossomed was awesome team spirit.

That year Bridget's hotel had one of the highest AOS scores in the region and the highest guest satisfaction scores in the country. It also reported the second-highest profit margin in the U.S.! When Bridget used this same model in her next job as regional director overseeing thirty Courtyard by Marriott hotels in three states, her region won all four of the annual super awards (Regional Director of the Year, Region of the Year, GM of the Year, and Hotel of the Year). The following year, her region won three of the four awards again and was the first ever to win Region of the Year back to back.

So how would Bridget sum up her advice to someone striving to be a roadrunner? "Value change and make change fun! Part of the process to change is reaching for the top in everything you do and realizing that you need others to get there. It's the people around you that make the miracles happen. If you help them realize their own greatness, the entire team moves to the next level. Fall in love," she says. "Nothing feels better than being in love. So why not fall in love with your staff, with the customers? This creates an environment where we really focus on each other as people and feel valued as individuals who make a difference for the team. Change and risk feel safe in a loving environment.

"And remember—we're not here for a long time; we're here for a good time!"

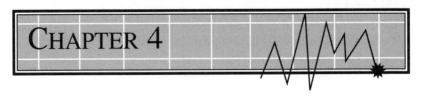

CHAPTER 4

Flock
Everyone Is a Full Player

The Road Runner is a solitary animal. But isn't business today about teams, partnerships, and alliances? Does that mean a roadrunner organization is simply an assemblage of people working on parallel, barely connected tracks? How do we square such opposing concepts?

Look very carefully at the Road Runner cartoons for clues to the nature of business relationships in the emerging economy. Every once in a while you see signs that the Road Runner is not operating alone at all. When he chooses to, he collaborates with someone, somewhere, to achieve an unexpected, extraordinary goal. That subtlety is part of his winning hand. His ability to link up with resources he does not "own" is so natural we barely notice it. We witness its impact.

Wile E. takes a big handful of Acme Guaranteed Slippery Axle Grease, rubs it on the bottom of his feet, and positions himself at the top of a steep hill. As the Road Runner comes zooming down the road, Wile E. races downhill like a skier. The Road Runner suddenly stops. Wile E. zooms by out of control, continuing right off a cliff. Ultimately, he lands on a stretch of railroad track and continues to ski, right into a tunnel. The last scene is the coyote pushing himself out of the tunnel trying to avoid a huge train bearing down hard at him. The view zooms up to the locomotive. The Road Runner is at the helm wearing an engineer's hat and a smile. Beep Beep!

Wile E. erects a beam to straddle two cliffs. Standing in the middle of the beam with a spear in hand, he ties himself to a rope that he has tied to the beam. Hearing a familiar "Beep Beep," he pushes off the beam, using it as leverage to create an arc like a pendulum, all the while holding his spear out to snare the approaching bird. Unfortunately, it's not the bird he thought he heard earlier. It's a huge truck that smashes into him. The last scene is a tight shot on the truck speeding away. Who's the driver? It's the Road Runner! He leans his head out of the window and sticks his tongue out. "Beep Beep!"

Where did the Road Runner get his vehicles? How did he get a driver's license? And where did he learn to drive? We'll never know the answers, but we do know this: The Road Runner does not operate all by himself. He knows people. The right people. And he periodically joins forces with them to do what needs to be done quickly, albeit temporarily. The Road Runner is connected.

The Road Runner is also tightly connected to his environment, unlike his adversary, who stands out like a sore paw. Roadrunners do not inhabit the desert; they are one with it. Camouflaged to blend with the landforms and foliage of the Southwestern outdoors, they can zoom about undetected by a menacing hawk overhead or a wily coyote on the ground. Their long skinny legs and sleek bodies enable them to streak across the desert floor with masterful agility. As one zoologist said of the funny-looking bird, "He's not only hard to catch; he's downright hard to see." Try as the Coyote may, he will never capture this bird. Why? Because he assumes the Road Runner is "just a bird," a simple morsel for the taking. But Wile E. is pursuing more than a mere bird; he's up against a whole system . . . bird, the bird's virtual partners, the desert. We call this powerful system: "flock."

"Flock" Means "The Power of One"

The emerging marketplace favors roadrunners, who are powerful players on their own and look to other powerful, capable allies for quick synergies. Technology today allows any of us to operate as sole proprietors connected to data, information, capital, people, and other resources around the world.

A friend of ours reminds us that a few years ago he was in front of his home computer terminal, viewing stock price fluctuations float across his screen. At the same time he was on the phone talking with his broker, who was in front of her terminal, looking at the same data. After a few buy-sell decisions, he suddenly blurted, "Hey, what do I need you for anyway?" He swears there was a ten-second silence. No one had ever said that to her before. She's no doubt learned (as the big brokerage firms are learning) that unless she starts offering innovative services and information that provide new value, she will be expendable.

A colleague of ours told us how he recently bought a new car, and it was one of the most pleasant experiences he's had in years. "Ninety-five percent of it took place in my living room," he explained. He logged onto Web sites and search engines to scan car sites around the country. He ferreted out the invoice prices dealers pay, examined a myriad of consumer data reports, and joined chat rooms. He downloaded software that allowed him to itemize the specifications he wanted and received a list of available cars meeting those specs in his e-mail box each morning. He located car brokers and followed up on a couple of deals over the phone.

The reason he said only 95 percent of it took place in his living room is that he eventually felt he actually had to try out his car of choice before he bought it—that was the last 5 percent! In the very near future, he predicts, decentralized virtual reality will make even that 5 percent unnecessary. He'll be able to do it all from his living room.

Does that sound ludicrously fantastic? Consider this: As late as 1977, both Ken Olsen, CEO of DEC, and Gordon Moore, CEO of Intel, were saying that they couldn't see any reason people would want to own personal computers in their homes. Yet, given the extraordinary developments in information technology since then, who's to say that financial services software packages in the near future won't have holographic images of Warren Buffett stepping out of our computers to sit down on our living room sofa to review our investment portfolio personally? Or how about one that would allow Tiger Woods to fine-tune our golf swing or the Surgeon General to perform our annual physical?

With the computing already available today, any single individual can operate as a knowledgeable, fully functioning business linked to allies around the world, or similarly, as an off-site but fully functioning contributor within a business enterprise. The fundamental truth is that "everyone is a full player." In fact, writers John Hagel and Marc Singer promise an emerging new role called "infomediaries"—third parties who help people find the best information for targeted needs and solutions.

"The Web has the promise of enabling everyone to reach far beyond the current corporate boundaries to compress space and time, to eliminate the middleman, and to provide better service at a lower cost through self-service," says Leonard Liu, CEO of financial software developer Walker Interactive Systems. In a 1998 interview with *Inc.* magazine, Chunka Mui, co-author of *Unleashing the Killer App,* observed that, "We're at the point now where the things that even big corporations are trying to catch up on are easily accessible to high school students." In other words, technology allows anyone access to anything and anyone.

Computing has become a social phenomenon. It used to be that computers were personal and isolated—you and your machine. Now the value of the computers is in connecting people. Roadrunners capitalize on this concept in order to form quick, virtual unions with the best talent anywhere on the planet. WWW means WORLD-WIDE web!

"The PC is just a blip," says Sun CEO Scott McNealy. "It's a big, bright blip, but still just a blip." Sun's Java technology is a key move toward supporting networks via a nonproprietary open-platform programming language. The new wave from Sun is Jini—a Java-based technology aimed at connecting anything electronic via the Web. Your computer will be tied to your kitchen appliances, TV, CD player, and telephones, allowing these devices to communicate with each other and enabling you to control the process remotely.

Consider the explosion in telecommuting, basement startups, and SOHOs (small-offices-home-offices). Guerrilla marketing guru Jay Levinson predicts that by the year 2001, one of every three American homes will have some sort of business operating from it. Like in Colorado Springs, where Mary Zalmanek does her day job at MCI and then operates her fast-growing Adventures of the Heart company from her home during weekends. Adventures of the Heart plans customized romantic adventures for clients looking for that special way to celebrate love and passion.

In response to this trend, Kinko's Copiers has dramatically boosted its revenue by redefining its core business from "copy center" to "full-service mobile office." Meanwhile, fast-growing HQ Systems provides full-service virtual offices to SOHOs, larger-company telecommuters, salespeople, roving project leaders, and others who wish to have a "downtown" corporate address for mail, phone messages, and periodic meetings without being tied down by a piece of property or an office payroll.

So here are Kinko's Copiers and HQ Systems, providing immediate access to state-of-the-art tools and technology to biz world roadrunners—just like those mysterious vendors of trucks and trains do to our avian counterpart in the cartoons.

What "the power of one" also means is that in the emerging Age of the Road Runner, the playing field will be level: Individuals armed with computers and networks will be able to compete with large organizations or ally with them as outside partners or employees—and they'll be able to do it as powerful, legitimate *full players*. This is not only a shift in wealth and prosperity, but also in cultural values and norms. Information technology and alliances will enable an individual to do more—to contribute more—in a week than some of today's behemoth corporations do in a month. Information, imagination, and speed will be an organization's greatest asset, and anyone with a computer and the ability to dream can become the CEO of their own job, if not their own organization.

In short, advancing technology gives small groups access to resources that once were the private domain of big ones. Networked computing, satellite feeds, and the Internet allow a tiny operation or an individual to draw from the knowledge base of much larger organizations around the world. Advances in information, communication, and transportation technology allow alliances and partnerships that can quickly transform a four-person start-up into a global player with serious clout. Little companies are no longer ma-and-pa yokel outfits; they're sophisticated and powerful. They are players.

Everyone Is a Player

A player is a person of action, one who is included and involved in a results-oriented activity that requires the use of personal skills. "Everyone is a player" implies both inclusion and outcome. While individual players may have strong egos, when they come together as a whole, the "flock" is egoless; the results startling. National Basketball Association athletes have been repeatedly labeled as selfish, egotistical, and irresponsible. Yet, during the 1990s, only three teams won the NBA world championship title: the Houston Rockets, the Chicago Bulls, and the San Antonio Spurs—all were flocks.

During their 1994 and 1995 championship drives, the Rockets strategy crafted by coach Rudy Tomjanovich was to submerge ego, individual stats, and personal gain in order to win as a team. "You have to be unselfish to get it done," says Rudy T. Or as *USA Today* newspaper columnist Bryan Burwell puts it: "You can have all those made-for-TV, chest-bumpin', 'I gotta get mine' superstars, but I'll take Tomjanovich's brand of players any day. He put together a team free of bad attitudes. He has sold everyone on the importance of being unselfish. Better to have hard-working solid citizens with ordinary games than brilliant talent with bone-headed destructive attitudes to bring down the fragile nature of team chemistry." This is pure roadrunner.

This also describes the Bulls under coach Phil Jackson. In Michael Jordan, Scottie Pippen, and Dennis Rodman, the Bulls had three of the strongest, most divergent egos one could imagine. Yet, under the tutelage of Coach Jackson, these three individuals, along with their teammates, were able to come together each season, in each game, and play as one. (In fact, it was only after now-retired superscorer Michael Jordan learned to create opportunities for others to score that Chicago was able to win its first title.) But once the season was over, indeed, once each game was over, Jordan and Rodman would go completely separate ways in pursuing their own interests. The Bulls were less of a team and more of a flock. They weren't the biggest or strongest—but they were fast, smart and played as one.

In any enterprise, people must be full players if they are to successfully give, share, and put in a championship perform-ance. There can be no benchwarming second-stringers, as there are on athletic teams. There can be no one treated as subordinate or expendable. In flocks, there are no ranks. Flocks are confederations of "ones," each with resources to share and ideas to champion. *Confederation* implies a sense of unity of purpose without letting the seams or side issues dis-tract. Flocks are egalitarian. They represent individual talents coming together to make something valuable happen.

This means the new definition of *value* (as in "value added," "shareholder value," or "value proposition") will have less to do with physical assets than with the capacity to connect and create synergy with others. Winning entities and successful individuals will be those who are best at picking, linking, and mobilizing ones to form the best flock. What would your worth to your organization be if it were based not on who you knew—or even *what* you knew—but on your ability to recruit (not hire) others to deliver their very best in a peer-managed, temporary endeavor?

Roadrunner leaders are adept at scouting talent and de-veloping teams. They are also crackerjacks at spotting redun-dant effort and, without fanfare, unshackling from the drag to go faster, with greater focus. They are constantly vigilant for "economies of sail," jettisoning anything that fails to add value or smooth the way. For service and resource providers, this means constantly reinventing value. "Forever" value is unlikely. And better to be valued intermittently than to be valued once and then abandoned for good.

Everyone Means *Every* One

Flock means everyone is valued as an equal player. And *everyone* means *every* one—the janitor, the clerk, the ring-nosed kid who works part-time in shipping or in solving your networked computing nightmares. It also means valued suppliers and partners who are so embedded in your operations that they are extensions of your organization. Excluding anyone from full participation is like starting the game with half the team still on the bench.

When Ron Patti took over the presidency of global supply management at communications hardware provider DSC Communications in 1997, he brought with him an entirely new mind-set on how to deal with suppliers. He communicated one simple message to all of them: "I assume we can count on you for top quality and on-time delivery. That's a given. What I'm really buying is your capabilities. I want you to figure out ways to help DSC reduce costs, boost sales, and be a better company. Don't just respond to our orders. Lead. Take us by the hand and show us better ways of running our company. Do that, and we'll do the same for you. Better still, you'll continue to grow—and grow with a bigger presence—in the DSC family."

The suppliers that we talked with applauded Patti's moves. In the new climate of open communication, full access, and collaboration, there can be no rewarding the procurement people for lying or jerking suppliers around just to save DSC a couple bucks. They eagerly "invested" in DSC with their best thinking and their key people and systems. By early 1998, Patti had already seen a difference: "In less than a year, we've gotten our suppliers to help us reduce our raw material inventory by $40 million, which is the equivalent of $200 million in sales."

Patti says the value-add also comes from unanticipated directions. A supplier who knew some key people in Germany made the appropriate introductions and helped DSC capture some lucrative distribution linkages in that country. From Patti's perspective, this is just part of a philosophy that says: No more pseudo-partnerships with vendors who can only supply commodity goods in a commodity transaction. "We need people who are excited about growing with us."

Working on Borrowed Brains

The roadrunner organization's primary asset is not its number of permanent employees. Instead it's the sheer number of contacts and networks among energetic, talented, powerful roadrunners who share information, expertise, ideas, imagination, and hard work. "The concept of the organization of the future," says PriceWaterhouseCoopers partner James Stalder, "will be firms of five." They will be temporary firms of five at that.

When retired Booz Allen–Hamilton chief Cyrus Freidheim writes about the "trillion dollar enterprise," he's not talking about a gargantuan, obscenely huge, multiple-megamerged enterprise. He's talking instead about a tight collaborative network of swift allied organizations, each a vital link in the production-supply-sales-service chain—total value of which approximates a trillion dollars.

Already we see movement in this direction, like the huge iridium project consortium, dedicated to the vision of freedom to communicate—anytime, anywhere. Spearheaded by Motorola, the iridium project is creating an expansive system of wireless global communication with a tight network of over 100 players, Kyocera, Raytheon, AlliedSignal, Bakrie, Sprint, and a slew of local telecommunications companies. Or, the growing alliance among Lucent Technologies, Motorola, Cisco Systems, and Nextel in developing DSP technology for next-generation applications and new markets. In the Age of the Road Runner, big, ponderous beasts that attempt to own everything outright via megamergers will become the slow, fat dodo birds losing ground to the thriving networked flocks of turbocharged roadrunner birds.

Increasingly, whether inside or outside the organization, the best minds are on loan—crossing functional, hierarchical, and even organizational boundaries in the process. And they are looking for fellow best minds—again, anywhere inside or outside the organization—to establish temporary, highly focused affiliations to accomplish some common goal. The name of the game is collaboration, creating trusting confederations of powerful, driven, full players, rather than the traditional scheme where nonpowerful "subordinates" work as permanent organizational "employees" to fulfill hierarchically imposed tasks and processes.

If the Road Runner were to ever stop moving long enough (and if he could say something other than "Beep Beep"), he'd describe the scene in terms of three premises:

Premise 1: We are all operating in a brain-based economy, where intangible assets like knowledge, intelligence, skills, and competencies are the crucial precursors of competitive advantage.

Premise 2: In a brain-based economy, you (and your company) cannot possibly collect all the best talent and intellectual resources outlined in Premise 1 under one roof, nor should you even try. No single organization—no matter how many mergers and acquisitions—can possibly corner the knowledge and talent market or even a fraction of it.

Premise 3: The solution, then, is threefold. First, figure out what you're world-class great in, or what you aspire to be world-class great in. Second, focus on that and invest heavily in it. Third, let go of everything else—divest it, sub it out, shut it down. Look to marry players around the world who are great at what you're not and who share your vision and values. In other words, seek to *access* the talent you don't

70

have. Work on borrowed brains, so to speak. Don't seek to own anything that's not relevant to your competitive success; resist the false allure of vertical integration, the "gotta own it" mind-set.

That said, the Road Runner would feel compelled to add a friendly little warning: Spend time carefully choosing an appropriate partner; then think about cultivating a "meaningful relationship" and maybe even growing old together. The best companies we've studied are increasingly reluctant to embrace some outside "partner" who merely meets the terms of a contract with commodity goods and services, even at a rock-bottom price. Increasingly, blue-chip organizations of all sizes—the Intels and DSCs of the world—are more interested in working long term with trustworthy suppliers who can apply their own expertise and resources to a wide range of operational and strategic opportunities. So it's not surprising that companies like health care products purveyor Baxter and plastics molder Nypro are drawn to each other. Baxter's philosophy is to prune down supplier lists and bring in the survivors as long-term partners, giving them training, sharing data and cost savings, and working collaboratively with them on common problems. As the supplier, Nypro's modus operandi is to build micro-facilities near its corporate customers, give them access to its databases, and encourage joint supplier-customer project teams to help each other slash lead time, inventory, space requirements, product inspections, and the like. That's the new breed of confederation: helping each other get better, not just meeting specs.

Access to resources is hot; ownership of resources is not! When Tom Peters exhorts, "Subcontract everything but your soul!" one meaning of *soul* is your core distinction. Roadrunners travel light, picking up and discarding resources along the road according to their needs. Coyotes stockpile and hoard. They merge with each other for bigger stockpiles. They brag about their full attics—imagine all the Acme stuff Wile E. has accumulated over the years! FTEs and head counts are the stuff prompting the coyote organization's arrogant smirks. No wonder roadrunner organizations pass the coyotes with ease.

Every Player Is FULLY Engaged

Fully has two important connotations. The first is bounty or abundance. Full players have all the necessary tools and opportunities, and they are familiar with everyone's responsibilities. They lie in an environment with easy access to ideas, information, resources, mentors, and growth. Full players stay full by continually growing and staying ever challenged. The implication for roadrunner leaders is obvious and important.

Fully also signifies being eligible or qualified. Full membership means complete rights without restrictions. Full player means "owner-like." And what a powerful lesson the Road Runner teaches us. The old model was straightforward: We joined a stable company, adapted to its routine and bureaucracy, kept our noses clean, and remained good soldier-lifers until retirement. Today, the roadrunner model is inexorably replacing that long-standing routine. *Authoritative* is replaced by *facilitative*; *in charge* now means "in tune." Leaders are facilitators, not power brokers or power mongers. Old-fashioned power (aka control) is irrelevant because "businesspeople" don't respond to dominance; they rise to opportunity.

The Danish company Oticon is two years ahead of its competition (including much larger players like Siemens and Panasonic) in the design and engineering of hearing aid technology and related high-margin end products. Recently retired CEO Lars Kolind has attributed his company's extraordinary growth over the past five years (double-digit growth in profitability) to an organization that he calls a "spaghetti structure."

Every employee at Oticon works on multiple projects. Hierarchy and functional structures have been nearly obliterated. People bring specific skills to the table (finance, marketing, human resources) but are expected to share those skills and learn from others while they pursue specific goals—be they internal cycle time reductions or external product line extensions. Projects are not hierarchically assigned; rather, strong, capable individuals choose to be members of specific project teams or are chosen by peers. Nor are project teams permanent; there is a constant, organic ebb and flow, as people move in and out of a project depending on its need. The "organization" is a writhing mass of projects. So is a person's "job."

We'll bet that if you examine every explosive growth company, be it an Internet company (like Yahoo!), a software company (like Red Hat), or a "hard" products company (like Oticon), you'll find an "everyone-a-full-player" spaghetti structure at the core. Even the most standard environments are steadily becoming more spaghetti and less "orderly." The alternative is extinction. Consider General Motors. Its Saturn facilities are a model of interdisciplinary, participative, culturally open environments. And with trusted "outsiders" like supplier Milacron, new spaghetti-like relationships with "outsiders" are being formed regularly. Cincinnati-based Milacron now provides full onsite chemical management for a number of GM facilities. Milacron people are on the shop floor, indistinguishable from GM employees. In fact, a number of hourly UAW GM employees report directly to Milacron folks.

Flock in Motion

In 1994 Oren formed a temporary project-oriented organization with Karen Sawyer of the American Management Association to produce a specific project: a marketable videotape on intelligent organizations that both Oren and AMA would profit from in the marketplace of ideas. Here is his event diary of the process:

For the last three months Karen Sawyer (in AMA's Boston office) and I (in my San Francisco area office) have been fleshing out concepts, scripts, contracts, mutual commitments, and timetables. We have never met face-to-face. It's all phone, fax, FedEx, and e-mail. For the next two months Karen and I work with Whit Rummel in North Carolina, who runs a small independent video production group called Allagash Productions, to do more concept work, line up companies to tape, and coordinate mutual commitments and timetables. I haven't met him yet.

Whit and his production crew go to three carefully chosen companies in different spots in the U.S.; Karen and I orchestrate the taping process, but we never go to the sites. It is all done through phone, fax, and e-mail. I still haven't met Karen face-to-face yet, or Whit.

At the same time Karen and I are working the same way with Nancy Praizler in Chico, California, who runs an independent training company. Nancy is going to write a training manual for the video. I haven't met her yet.

April 1995; After months of working closely "together," Karen, Whit, and I meet for the first time at dinner, when I fly into Boston on the evening of August 10 to prepare for our taping the next day.

Twenty-four hours later: Everyone has disbanded. We'll do the wrap-ups, including "meetings" with the sales force, through mail and conference calls. What's left? A videotape and manual [which won outstanding ratings in excellence and were a solid marketplace success—the video was ultimately bought by CRM Films]. Just as important, we now have a network of intelligence and talents that any one of us can draw upon in the future, a set of enduring personal and professional relationships that would be an asset to all sorts of future projects.

Peter Drucker once said that the only time he ever witnessed anything significant occur in an organization was when it was pushed by "a monomaniac with a mission"—which is a good characterization of our Road Runner. In most cases, however, a monomaniacal roadrunner joins forces with others who share a similar mania; they know they can't do it alone.

Wile E. places a small piece of railroad track across the road and adds bushes at each end for camouflage. He then stands in the road disguised with a hat and beard, ringing a bell and holding a "RR Stop" sign. The Road Runner runs right over Wile E., knocking him onto the track. Suddenly the sound of a train approaching pierces the air. Wile E. looks up just in time to get flattened by the train. Seeing stars, he slowly pulls his battered body up. Lo and behold, he sees the Road Runner relaxing in the caboose as the train pulls away. Beep Beep!

Just like Oren and his videotape buddies, roadrunners naturally seek temporary, mutually enhancing configurations where they can work hard and creatively with fellow soul mates toward the attainment of extraordinary goals. Roadrunners instinctively seem to start up companies as entrepreneurs or start up projects within companies as entrepreneurs or champions, like those hardy, driven souls who obsessively pushed their dreams like Post-it notepads, disposable diapers, and Miata roadsters. Or, Matt Damon and Ben Affleck—two struggling actors who had nothing—scratching and scrounging to create the movie *Good Will Hunting*.

After futilely chasing the Road Runner while wearing a pair of Fleet Foot Jet Propelled Tennis Shoes, an exhausted Wile E. decides to hide behind a billboard next to the highway, holding an axe in hand. When he hears the "Beep Beep" he's been waiting for, he runs out into the middle of the road and raises the axe. Unfortunately, the source of the Beep Beep is a big bus, which comes barreling down the road and flattens him. The dazed, beat-up Wile E. raises his head and sees in the back window of the bus the smiling Road Runner, propping up his head on his hand, raising his eyebrows, sticking out tongue, "Beep Beeping," and finally pulling down the window shade.

Roadrunners are more than willing to work collaboratively, but they work best in flocks, not packs. This is an important point. Remember we said the best minds are the ones on loan? Those whose minds are not on loan often seem more comfortable as part of a conforming, hierarchical "pack." They have pack needs.

Packs are for coyotes! As we know from studying the coyote's cousin, the wolf, packs have a tightly defined social hierarchy with dominants and submissives—just like conventional organizations. Packs suggest "teams," where conformity is the greatest virtue and the emphasis in *team player* is usually on *team*, not on *player*. To be part of a team in many organizations, one must give up individuality, obstreperousness, and mania. "Teams" in many organizations also mean mind-numbing dialogues in mediocrity, soul-less meetings, endless bureaucratic entanglements, and bland, vanilla interpersonal relationships that dilute creative conflict and personal accountability.

Roadrunners don't run in packs; they're wary of conventional "teams." When roadrunners seek synergy, they operate best in flocks. Flocks are made up of independent birds that bring themselves together for a specific purpose. In a flock environment, someone may champion a project, but nobody is an alpha bird like the lead dog in a pack. In a flock, you see mutual respect, mutual sharing of authority as needed, and continually fluid job titles and responsibilities, including who is best suited to be leader this week.

The Roadrunner Leader
of the Flock

Newspaper editor Bob Stromberg describes the surprise he felt as a boy when, lying on his back in a field, he saw "the head goose, the leader of the 'V' formation, suddenly swerve out, leaving a vacancy that was promptly filled by the goose behind. The former leader then flew alongside the formation and took its place in the back of the line, and *they never missed a beat!*"

As Stromberg explains the leadership dynamics of a flock, "When the head goose grabs that wind, air is displaced which promptly rushes up again to reclaim its space, only to meet the smiling face of the bird flying behind whose wings just happen to be in the downward position; a very precarious position. But, it doesn't last for long because that upward rush gives him a push and he's right back up there where he belongs. That bird then grabs the air again causing another upward rush which helps the bird behind, and so it goes on down the line. The head bird shields the wind and all the rest are carried by him or her, by varying degrees of course, from the back which is best, to the front which is worst. And when the head goose has had enough, he or she simply falls back and relies on another bird for strength, when strength is what it lacks.

"That is how a goose can fly from way up North, to way down South and back again. But he cannot do it alone, you see. It is something which he needs to do in community."

Flocks are never leaderless. They simply have a concept of leader that is not based on job title, charm, force, or tenure. Leadership comes from anyone, anytime, and it goes to anyone, anytime. It is rejected when it inhibits flow; it is valued when it fosters flow and unleashes power. The leader's role is to be a release valve, not a restraining force; a conduit, not a source of power. Roadrunner leaders are helpers—they are resources to make the enterprise focused and efficient. They facilitate, meaning they help make things easy. Leaders not only encourage; they invite others to join in the cheerleading. When the head goose begins to honk, it triggers a chorus of honking. The sounds are more than bird talk; they bolster connection and instill camaraderie.

The strength of roadrunner leaders comes from their commitment to the mission and their devotion to the flock. Devotion implies dedication, not necessarily affection. Roadrunner leaders lead out loud: They say what they believe and encourage others to do likewise. Secrets are taboo; candor is lauded. They know people can't act like owners if they aren't treated like owners. And that means full disclosure and open communication.

Jack Stack, CEO of Springfield ReManufacturing, started an open book management revolution by sharing key company information with all employees. First, he worked at driving fear out of the workplace. Second, he trained employees in business literacy, which gave them the tools to understand the economics of the business and an appreciation for how unit costs related to company margins. He altered the compensation system to give employees a larger share of company profits. Finally, he shared with all employees the same data business owners want, including all financials. Suddenly, Springfield workers were asking for more information about customers and policing each other about waste and excess as they took the CEO view, rather than looking at results through the narrow prism of their own unit. Stack firmly believes that Springfield ReManufacturing's phenomenal success is the result of creating a company of roadrunner businesspeople and flocks headed by virtual leaders who earned their positions rather than having them handed from top down.

Roadrunner leaders know that full players only stay full if they are perpetually replenished with skills and knowledge. Roadrunner leaders are mentors to the flock and all its members. They sponsor and encourage networks for learning, both inside and outside the organization. They perpetually bring in resources to keep the flock sharp and up-to-date. They squeeze a learning component out of each assignment, always debriefing with an eye toward learning and improvement. Asking "What did you learn?" is just as important as "What went right or wrong?" They enable team members to share individual insights with the entire group. Roadrunner leaders are just as ardent learners as they are teachers.

Here is a final thought on how a roadrunner flock can create havoc for coyotes:

Wile E. Coyote has bought a large catapult, and he now places a large boulder into the contraption for a slingshot effect. Holding the trip rope, standing just to the right of the catapult, he waits for the Road Runner. When the bird runs by, Wile E. pulls the rope, but the catapult does not work. In fact, the boulder falls the wrong way, crushing him. So he tries again. Nothing. Again. No luck. Again. Nada. Finally, he climbs to the top of the catapult and pushes against the rock in an attempt to loosen it. The catapult suddenly springs, sending the boulder and Wile E. flying through the air right through a rock tower, carving out a silhouette of coyote as he punches through. The flattened coyote, still clinging to the flying boulder, collides with electrical wires. The wires act like a rubber band, stopping his forward momentum, then catapulting Wile E. and the boulder straight back through the air in the opposite direction, through the rock tower again. Wile E. lands back in his original spot, the boulder drops straight down on him, crushing him once again. The camera then zooms onto a small label on the original "defective" catapult: "Built by the Road Runner Manufacturing Company." A picture of the Road Runner attached to the side of the contraption then comes to life. The bird "Beep Beeps" and runs off. That's all, folks!

BIRDSEED

- Eliminate titles, pecking order, hierarchy, anything that smacks of a pack. Think of "rank" as connoting something with an odor, not something to be saluted!
- Help all players access whomever they need, whatever information they need, whenever needed. Create an open-door, informal, egalitarian, no-buffer culture.
- Encourage people to form temporary affiliations with other powerful full players—customers, suppliers, strategic partners—to achieve exceptional goals.
- Help everyone think and act like an owner: "What would I do, and with whom would I connect, if I owned this enterprise?"
- Bash myths, ban secrets, and squash rumors. Appoint a "down with secrets" group to hunt down barriers to openness. Rotate membership.
- Make sure performance assessments, career advancement, rewards, and bonuses are contingent on cross-unit collaboration, not individual or unit contribution.

Tail Feathers: A Roadrunner on a Harley

Brian Hulse is six feet one, weighs 265 pounds, wears his hair in a ponytail, occasionally plays lead guitar in a local country-rock band, and carries a photo of his Harley-Davidson motorcycle in his wallet. He is also a manager in the West Coast branch of Destec Operating Company, a Bakersfield, California, company that develops, builds, and maintains co-generation plants.

Brian's education consists of a high school diploma, twelve college credits of music and computer science, and ten years in the Navy. His experience in management was nil before joining Destec, which hired Brian in 1988 as a technical specialist for gas turbine maintenance in a nonmanagement capacity. But Brian soon became restless; he found the job too limiting.

So while performing his official duties, he began to circulate through the company asking people, "How can I help? Is there anything I can work on for you?" People who ordinarily would have been skeptical of such advances were disarmed by his sincerity. Besides, he had expertise they could use.

"I tried to let people know that I wanted to help them be successful too," Brian recollects. That meant not only problem-solving with them, but getting them to open up and trust him with their concerns. It even meant pushing them out of their comfort zones toward new solutions to messy technical and systems problems.

Gradually, people began to invite Brian to brainstorming sessions and project meetings. As time passed, he became increasingly valuable to more and more people in the company. On his own initiative, he started an internal project to create a central service turbine maintenance team that could troubleshoot in any Destec facility. Although Brian was the official head of the team, he made it a point to quickly "grow" a new leader for the group. Once everything was functioning smoothly, Brian moved on, and the team became a permanent fixture in the organization.

By this point, top management was taking notice of this strange, brash character who seemed to be everywhere. The West Coast management team began to invite him to its meetings. By 1993,

Brian was involved in various projects relating to strategy, marketing, technology transfer, and capital budgeting. He was a busy man, even flying to New Zealand to work with a key vendor on a million dollar project.

By 1998, Brian had numerous projects under his belt, as well as a history of three job titles. For three years, he had been an operations and maintenance manager, initially for three plants, then for nine. He then became the coordinator of a team developing a strategic plan for a new Destec parts company, a responsibility that he took on for about a year. He then moved on to be California services manager for purchasing and warehousing, a position he held until early 1998.

"Now," he laughed when we spoke to him in mid-1998, "I don't have a job." What he meant was no job title, no job description, no employees reporting to him, no secretary, no career path. So what do you do? we asked. "Well," he pondered, "I report directly to Mark Voss, the President of Destec. I hang out and look for things to do. And then I borrow people to help me get them done."

The man is pure roadrunner. He's always on the move, never in one spot, never staying long in one official "job." He's in tune with his environment, continually sniffing out opportunities to add value. He's constantly experimenting, always resourceful, always looking ahead. He was never "given" his "job," nor did he feel entitled to it. He just acted as a full player from the beginning, and eventually people started to treat him as one.

Instinctively, Brian acted as if all boundaries were permeable and the enterprise was virtual. He crossed functional lines and structural boundaries from the start—and didn't ask permission. He assumed that whatever he did would not be permanent or routine; in fact, he made sure that wouldn't happen. He created a virtual environment for himself.

He was, and is, passionate about learning. Seeking mentoring, mentoring others, volunteering for new experiences, mastering new skills—that's Brian's MO. In fact, when we first met him in 1992 he was attending—on his own initiative—a multiday management seminar. Over the years, he's built up an enviable intellectual asset base, making himself more valuable within Destec and more marketable outside the company.

When we asked Brian to describe his work philosophy, he ticked off flexibility, continuous learning, and big-picture thinking as key components:

"I think it's important to be flexible, not get hung up on titles and job descriptions. I see myself as a shortstop on a major league baseball team. I roam left and right, forward and back; I'm there to make the great plays, to fill the hole fast. . . . You gotta keep learning. If you're interested in just one function or one task, you won't go far. Companies nowadays want people to be good at a lot of things; the more you learn about the business as a whole, the more opportunities you'll have.

"It's important to think big. When I was services manager, I saw that some of the people who reported to me were accepting a 3 percent cost reduction goal in one project. That seemed reasonable; it's what the company was expecting. But I knew the business pretty well by then, and I figured that the company needed more like a 40 percent reduction, and I believed that if we worked together as a team, we could pull it off. We did."

Sounds like you feel empowered, we suggested.

Brian frowned: "You know, Voss may be the President, but he doesn't have 'power' to give me. He gives me 'stretch' assignments, he trusts me, and he lets me do them. That means a lot."

So what does the future hold for you?

"I don't have a clue."

Are you at all concerned with this ambiguity? The lack of an official job?

"A little," Brian confesses. "But I have confidence in this company, and in a worst-case scenario, I have confidence in my ability to find something else."

He shouldn't have to worry about that. Roadrunner CEOs like Glen Tullman are looking for him desperately.

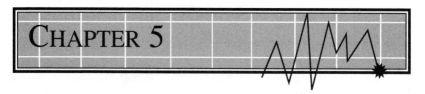

Chapter 5

Freedom
All Boundaries Are Permeable

The Road Runner is liberty incarnate . . . moving all over the desert with freedom. Even if Wile E. puts up a picture of a highway on the edge of a ravine, the Road Runner just runs through it unimpeded by any sense of boundary or barrier. Putting roadrunners behind restrictive fences (aka narrow job descriptions, mindless policies, obsessive hierarchical controls, etc.) risks turning them into barnyard chickens. Most will "fly the coop" long before they are domesticated, going to your competition or starting their own company!

Wile E. Coyote, on the other hand, perpetuates his self-en-slavement by choosing the security of dependence over the unpredictability of freedom. He creates his own boundaries with his obsessive plans, his acute myopia, and his sloppy execution, all of which do him in, even when the Road Runner is not around. As for so many of his counterparts in the business world, the coyote's more-of-the-same thinking is the most self-destructive, self-imposed boundary to success possible.

Wile E. Coyote sets up a fake railroad crossing. He goes over to a record player, carrying a record entitled "Railroad Crossing Sounds. Hi Fi." He starts playing the sounds. When the Road Runner runs up to the "railroad crossing," Wile E. jumps onto the tracks right in front of him. Suddenly a train barrels down the tracks and runs Wile E. over. The Road Runner, who hasn't moved an inch all this time, just stands there watching the train.

Domesticated employees may occasionally bark, but they have forgotten how to roar. They may occasionally sniff the air for adventure, but they long ago lost the taste of unbridled passion or the rush of cutting-edge pioneerism. They stay in their sheltered stalls, their cozy cubicles, their predictable paradigms. A paper cut is a major wound. Some dream, most become numb, all relinquish their nature for certainty and stability. Entitlement is the sound of long-term domestication. So is dullness. Former 3M CEO Lew Lehr put it well: "If you place too many fences around people they can easily become pastures of sheep. And how many patents are assigned to sheep?" Roadrunners smile because they are free; coyotes look grim because they are not free.

Wile E. is hiding under a manhole cover, with a sneer on his face, holding a grenade. He hears "Beep Beep" so he pulls the pin on the grenade. The Road Runner runs up but takes a different road, going above where Wile E. is hiding. As the Road Runner runs by, a rock is pushed over the side, landing right onto the manhole cover. The Coyote can't lift the cover. Boom! The manhole cover and rock are propelled straight up. Haggard-looking, Wile E. raises himself out of the manhole only to have the cover land on his head—followed by the rock.

In the Age of the Road Runner, boundaries melt; knowledge and people flow freely, respecting no borders. Everything migrates—information, people, capital—and no country, company, or person can stop it. Advances in hardware and software, electronic linkages, the World Wide Web, globalization, deregulation, outsourcing, customer pull, alliances, cross-pollination, interdisciplinary teams, employee migration—all contribute to a constant mobility and a convergence of ideas, people, products, and processes. This river can't be dammed, not even by the biggest, most powerful coyotes in the world. Roadrunners ride this wild, untamable river with glee.

The Structure of Freedom

Hierarchical structures are not an essential tool for mobilizing collective energy; they are simply a convenient one. The concept of organizational structures and boundaries was crafted to meet a specific need at a particular time; they served a vital and important purpose. However, like many compelling ideas of old, as times change the concept outlives its usefulness. As a fish is the last to know it is in water, those who continue to cling to the concept of structure begin to assume it is inherent and therefore obligatory. They assume that the antithesis of organizational boundaries and structure is chaos and anarchy.

Organizational structures have historically been the source of order and discipline among ancient armies of the world. Command and control beat back many a pagan mob! Peter Drucker notes that business in the latter 1800s copied the command and control structure of the Prussian army because it was the most successful organization of the day. This military model was later perfected by Alfred P. Sloan, CEO of General Motors, who created an orderly and predictable bureaucracy. At GM, units made up departments, which made up divisions, which made up groups. All this made sense when the terrain was characterized by a small finite group of vendors; limited customer choice; and product standardization for mass markets and bulk, routine, and economies of scale as key strategic drivers.

Hierarchical structure was a convenient way to mobilize humans who responded obediently to rank as they carried out well-organized, tightly planned tasks. Military heroes like Patton, Eisenhower, and Bradley were held up as leadership prototypes for bosses to model. Managers managed by objectives (with an emphasis on the *object* end of that word). They relied on standard operating principles and written policies to dictate action, reaction, and new action. They were schooled in ways to plan, organize, direct, and control effectively. Leaders were more sensitive to rank than competence. People looked up for leadership; leaders looked down at the rank and file. The physical and psychic distance between the CEO and the front-line employee was as vast as that between the general and the private.

If the Road Runner were a consultant, he'd tell us, "Think of your unit as a great start-up!" Great start-ups are permeable. In start-ups, there are few preconceived notions or hardened ideas. People talk directly to the people they need to talk to, go directly where they need to go, and connect to whatever data they need. There are some boundaries, but they are limited. More importantly, in start-ups people show the boundaries healthy disrespect. The CEO is on a first name basis with the temporary receptionist and will  help collate and staple a rush document needed by a customer. Unfortunately, once the organization is successful, leaders too often forget who "brung 'em to the dance." They say, "Let's get organized," forgetting that it was that fluid, fermenting chaos that created their success in the first place. Soon, the trappings of control and hierarchy emerge, and a whole slew of organizational and interpersonal boundaries begin to crop up. Roadrunner organizations try to mow down as many boundaries as possible. They don't allow anarchy, but they also understand that the apparent messiness and disorder of permeability is a natural part of breakthrough thinking and action.

Permeability is the roadrunner way to utilize brains, share expertise and skills, expand the conversation. By "expand the conversation," we mean bringing in fresh people (who are unconcerned with or unaware of "how we always do things here") and fresh ideas (à la "what if?" and "why not?"). By expanding the conversation, organizations avoid staying locked into the same old patterns, in which industry people talk to industry people, in-house people talk to in-house people, marketers talk to marketers, and top management isolates itself on mahogany row, speaking only to one another and a few consultants. Through an expanded conversation, we invite new possibilities and enrich fresh perspectives.

A Skirmish, Not a Fight

We have all grown up with the adage "Don't fight battles you can't win." Roadrunners observe another rule: "Don't fight battles that shouldn't be fought." Since boundaries are not really real, roadrunners don't waste time fighting them; they just ignore them. Like that middle manager who ignores lines of communication and goes right to the person she needs to talk to. Like that project leader who bypasses the step-by-step procedures to get a pilot project functioning quickly. Like Steve Jobs and Scott McNealy leaving Hewlett-Packard to start Apple Computer and Sun Microsystems, respectively, because their dream was being squashed in-house.

We see a beam of wood between two cliffs with a pulley system and a 10,000-pound weight attached with a rope. Wile E. is off to the side holding the end of the rope. The Road Runner runs down the road. The Coyote times it and then pulls the rope, undoing a latch. Wile E. smirks. Nothing happens. Wile E. gets angry, clenches his fists, and runs after the Road Runner. But now the weight falls and the audience hears the weight hit Wile E. He walks back into the picture, flat as a pancake with a tail and two legs sticking out.

Roadrunners streak across the desert of enterprise without paying homage to fences or cattle guards. Any policy, structure, role, or relationship that represents an inefficient use of energy is "ignored to death." The Road Runner way is not to fight, fuss, or flee but rather to move to a higher plane. Roadrunners are not warriors in the adversarial sense or worriers in the pessimistic sense. Roadrunners are about gleeful soaring. Even though they never actually fly, psychologically they are lighter than other birds.

Roadrunners Are Boundary Hunters

With today's technology, boundaries are irrelevant. Time and distance are collapsed. Anyone can access anyone and anything—disregarding time, space, or stature—through groupware, intranets, and expert systems. Roadrunner organizations like Sun Microsystems, Oticon, VeriFone, Allscripts, Pixar, and Buckman Labs are places where anyone can e-mail anyone, exchange documents with anyone, access the company's financial/manufacturing/marketing, etc., database anytime, hunt down any piece of knowledge, or find out who knows what, using an in-house electronic knowledge network/electronic "yellow pages"—all by just pointing and clicking on a browser.

Organizations like Sun, Ford, IBM, and Caterpillar have created "collaboratories" of scientists and engineers in separate locales, who work in real-time together on product development and design via televiewers, videoconferencing, shared computer displays and whiteboards, networked electronic notebooks, and synchronized Web browsers. The term *collaboratory* was coined by William Wulf when he worked at the National Science Foundation. It was invented to mean "a center without walls in which the nation's researchers can perform their research without regard to geographical location—interacting with colleagues, accessing instrumentation, sharing data and computational resources, and accessing information in digital libraries." Change "nation's researchers" to "anyone" and "research" to "work" and you capture the spirit of permeability for any function or task.

Roadrunner organizations use electronic connections (EDI, shared databases, extranets) with vendors, suppliers, distributors, customers, sales forces, and subsidiaries around the world to transcend boundaries and insure real-time response. Breaking down barriers not only allows real-time consumer profiling and data mining; it enables one-to-one response to market units of one person. "We are seeing the networking of the world," says Netscape's Mark Andreesen, "as the interconnecting of all businesses and a growing number of individuals creates a seamless electronic web."

But again, culture (not technology) is the ultimate killer of useless boundaries. AES is an independent producer of electric power based in Arlington, Virginia. With over 6,000 employees, they have no corporate departments for legal, HR, and operations purchasing, and there are only thirty people at "headquarters." Power is pushed down; people at all levels make key decisions. All information is public and accessible; associates are treated like business professionals. "If all information about finance goes to finance," says CEO Dennis Bakke, "and all information about legal matters goes to the legal department, it's impossible to get well-rounded people who can think about the whole world." AES had a 1998 market value of over $6 billion!

Another example: An employee may easily see the need to reduce the lag time between customer orders and delivery of the product. But to devise a plan, to fix the problems, he or she needs information about inventory control, logistics, current costs, the impact of delivery time on cash flow, and the bearing of the current order cycle on customer satisfaction. The technology is already there to do this. It's the boundaries of structure and habit that block the flow. The permeability of organizational boundaries is not just an issue of technology and structure. It has also to do with culture—and especially with trust.

Roadrunners Rely on Trust

Trust is the fuel that makes permeability work. Trust is the glue that holds people together as they work in ambiguous, uncertain roles—within even more ambiguous, uncertain times. Without trust, goals like empowerment and open communication fall far short of their potential; they may even become caricatures of their intent, just another "this year's program." Go a step further: Study any organization or unit marked by high internal distrust, and you will see an organization in decline—regardless of its technology, regardless of its robust balance sheet, marketing pizzazz, or high-priced CEO.

Why? Because if we can't assume that we all operate with the same values and purpose, if we can't count on each other during the tough times, if we can't work together with candor, honesty, mutual respect, and genuine win-win collaboration, then we might as well accept second-class status as an organization—regardless of the next sexy merger or technology purchase.

When Amazon.com launched their new online auction service they led with boldness and trust. In a letter to Amazon.com customers, Founder and CEO Jeff Bezos wrote: "We're doing something unusual with Amazon.com Auctions . . . we're guaranteeing buyers a safe auction experience—and we're doing it on the honor system. . . . Fraud will be rare, but the Amazon.com Auctions Guarantee means that if it does happen to you, it's our problem. Essentially, we're going to take your word for it if you're ever the victim of fraud."

Unfortunately, discussions about increasing trust too often revolve around strictly interpersonal dimensions like "How can I break down my inner barriers to communicating openly with you?" or "How might your team and my team let go of our negative stereotypes of each other?" The interpersonal dimensions are all worthwhile, but they put a low ceiling on where we need to go. AT&T Vice President William Moody says that trust, or the lack of it, is embedded in the very way we run our enterprises: "Either you build systems that unleash trust or you build systems that diminish trust." All too often, it's the latter. Many of our internal structures, policies, and procedures send a damaging—and damning—message that people are fundamentally unworthy of trust. They suggest to us, "Of course we trust you, but . . ." Moody is correct on one other vital point: It's either-or. Either you and your organization trust and are trustworthy . . . or not. Either you trust your spouse, and your spouse trusts you, or you don't. Period. Gray is a cop-out. Tell your spouse "I kind of trust you" and see the reaction you get.

A Study in Trust

One of Oren's MBA research assistants told a revealing story about his boundary-permeability experience while an intern at Sun Microsystems' public policy department. Here are the ingredients for his little tale: "John" (he prefers that we not identify him) is a student intern, he's a temporary employee, and he's working part-time. As you read the following vignette, ask yourself about the status and expectations (aka trust) that your organization affords to someone in the position of a part-time student "temp."

Sun's public policy department follows national and state issues that might have an impact on the computer industry, such as encryption, Internet regulation, immigration, and environmental affairs. A Public Policy Forum headed by the department director meets monthly to review relevant trends and opportunities. An issue that deserves further exploration is taken over by an issue manager and an issue executive. The issue manager is anyone at any level who has an interest in the topic. The issue executive—who is a top manager in the company—provides policy guidance and will act when necessary on behalf of the company.

Keep in mind that these meetings revolve around very sensitive public policy discussions. Corporate capabilities, strategies, and alternative courses of action are reviewed openly. As a member of the department, John (the "temp") was invited to participate in these critical meetings. As it turns out, John had a particular interest in helping the manager of the Internet regulation issue—which covered areas like Internet taxation, First Amendment rights, and privacy. That he did, but he went a step further.

John's major concern was that Sun was not acting quickly enough on these issues. So, in his words: "I came up with the idea of an Internet Regulation Rapid Response Team. The IRRRT would not meet regularly, only when there was a hot issue.

"In order to implement this, I needed the approval of the issue executive, who in this case was the president of JavaSoft, Alan Baratz. I drew up a rough plan, had it quickly reviewed by the public policy director and the issue manager, and then sent it over to Alan Baratz. I then called his office and set up a time to meet with him. What I did is like an intern in General Motors' marketing department calling the president of the Buick division for a meeting. The Public Policy director and I met with Baratz and his PR person, and he agreed to go ahead with my plan."

An intern being invited to sensitive discussions? A "temp" calling up a senior executive and then meeting with him? What's the world coming to? And if that's not enough, here's the punch line: It was determined that John would lead Sun Microsystems' Internet Regulation Rapid Response Team. Pretty typical of most organizations, right? Are you surprised to learn that Sun asked John to stick around after the summer and that he worked for them throughout his MBA tour-of-duty at University of San Francisco?

Sun trusted John's intelligence, innovation, and initiative.

From the very beginning—when CEO Scott McNealy, wearing shorts, met with all the summer interns to discuss company philosophy—John was treated like a full member of the Sun family. He had access to passwords that allowed him immediate entrée to Sun's intranet (which includes a myriad of corporate marketing, financial, and human resource data), as well as to the 30,000 in-house Web pages that provide information on everything from products, technology, safety programs, substance abuse, and business philosophy. John was encouraged, even expected, to get whatever information he needed and to go visit whomever he needed to visit, anytime, anywhere. The entire environment reeked trust. Because of that, John was able to see a need and develop a plan (if you're fenced in by boundaries, you don't see a need and you certainly don't develop a plan; those responsibilities are someone else's job). At Sun, John operated in an open environment that creates intellectual fermentation, that fuels over two million in-house e-mail messages per day, that captures the imagination of the best and brightest (from Java creator James Gosling to razor-sharp MBAs like John), and ultimately allows Sun to shine in the high-tech battleground.

The 2 Percent Jerk Factor

One last word. In promoting permeability, we are not advocating blind, naive trust. AT&T's Moody is a veteran of too many telecommunication wars to be a fool. He knows that it's a harsh desert out there, and he knows that not everybody on earth (or at AT&T) is trustworthy. But what sets him and folks at Sun apart from the others is that he begins with the assumption that people are trustworthy . . . until they prove otherwise. Why start with the premise that John—just because he's not a full-time executive-level employee with 200 years of experience—is not worthy of being involved in sensitive corporate matters?

A few years ago, we heard Keith Dunn, then CEO of McGuffy's restaurant chain, put the matter in vivid terms. His workforce consists of busboys, bartenders, maître d's, waiters, plus back-office support personnel. Dunn thinks that at best 2 percent of his workforce might be lazy or dishonest, so he asks himself a simple question: Why would I want to create an organization that basically tells the 98 percent who are hardworking, honest people that I suspect *them* of being lazy and dishonest too? Why would I want to treat everyone the way I would treat the 2 percent?

We've called this assumption the 2 Percent Jerk Factor. Maybe 2 percent of your people are jerks. Maybe. They're not trustworthy. If you're smart, however, you'll absorb them and treat everyone as if they were the 98 percent that aren't your jerks, but your allies. If you're even smarter, you'll let the 2 percent jerks expose themselves in your wide-open environment and then you'll remove them quickly and unapologetically, regardless of their degrees, pedigrees, or tenure.

The Roadrunner Leader and the Landscape of Freedom

Permeability does not start with dismantling organizational structures; it begins with leadership attitudes. Freeing up the organization starts with freeing up how we view our role. The only boundaries that are honored and nurtured are those that meet a leadership need, not an organizational one. To become roadrunner leaders we must recast our own view of freedom and better understand the internal impediments to permeability.

Freedom comes through a subtraction process, not addition. Liberation is the act of taking away organizational rules and structures which depress speed, agility, and imagination. Liberation is the act of removing constraints that inhibit people's ability or willingness to take initiative and accountability. The spirit of freedom lies innate within each of us. It is asserted whenever barriers are removed.

Wile E. Coyote may have an embryonic free spirit deep within him. But his greed and conceit rob him of the unrestrained delight personified (birdified!) by the Road Runner. Wile E. shows us three countenances: the doggedness of pursuit, the sneer of covert activity, and the agony of defeat. There is never the carefree boundary-less rapture we see practically every time the Road Runner is on the scene. Wile E. is obsessed; the Road Runner is free!

Boundary Bashing Is a Personal Mission

What attitudinal obstacles keep Wile E. leaders from running free like the Road Runner? The comical contest between our two characters can teach us much about the very different psychological landscapes in which each operates. Even when no organizational boundaries are present, arrogance, aimlessness, ignorance, and fear can inhibit the coyote's freedom. Freedom inside is just as crucial to the roadrunner's essence as freedom without.

From Arrogance to Humility . . .

It would never occur to a roadrunner to be arrogant. Arrogant leaders focus on either the past or their image, caught up in what they were or what they seem. Roadrunners are more interested in what they can be. Their forward-looking nature keeps them forever filled with awe, not weighted down by history or image. Roadrunner organizations are numerator thinkers, increasing value through careful addition and wise alteration. And Wile E. Coyote? His business card tells the story . . . Wile E. Coyote, Genius!

We see a box with the label: "One Acme Batman's Outfit." Wile E. dons the green body suit with mask—only his snout sticks out. He raises his arms to reveal wings. As the music swells we watch the Coyote perched on the edge of a cliff dive toward the canyon floor. As he falls, he begins to flap his wings. Just before smashing to the ground, Wile E. swoops horizontally and then begins to gain altitude. He takes a couple of confident loops. We see Wile E. proudly flying, chest out, back arched, eyes closed as he continues to flap his wings and gain speed. He looks directly at the audience with a smirk as if to say "I am a world-class flying ace." Still looking at the audience he smashes into the side of a mountain and falls to the canyon floor.

From Aimlessness to Purpose . . .

Freedom comes from purposeful action. And roadrunners succeed because they are full of purpose. Wile E. gets entangled in his myopic, obsessive microgoal. He never considers a grander, loftier perspective. Because he stays low to the ground, he not only misses important opportunities; he makes himself a victim of his surroundings. Roadrunners are always clear on their overall aim and are allies with their surroundings.

We all work more confidently when we feel a part of an important mission. We also make more responsible decisions. FedEx chairman Fred Smith reminds FedEx employees of their purpose or mission: "You aren't just 'taking stuff by 10:30 A.M.' You transport the most precious cargo in the world—an organ for a vital transplant, a gift for a special ceremony, a factory part that may have halted a company."

Aimlessness occurs when the organization's mission or purpose is not sufficiently compelling. We get sidetracked, like going to the library to research a project and getting distracted by a stack of old *Life* magazines. Roadrunners pursue only missions with magnetic appeal. If distraction comes easily, they reassess the mission, generally trading it in for a more gripping one. Drift also comes from a lack of discipline. Roadrunners are never lazy.

When all is said and done, roadrunner organizations go beyond boundaries by leapfrogging the usual idea of mission: They inspire a shared cause, a crusade. By this we mean they have a vision of what the company is about—what it's trying to do—that is inspirational, universally understood and accepted, and, most important, exceptional, even paradigm-shaking, in its potential impact. Investigate organizations as diverse as Nike, Starbucks, Microsoft, Sun, Dell, Ritz-Carlton, Harley-Davidson, Swatch, Enron, E*Trade, CNN, and ESPN, and you will find that they explicitly stand for something unique, special, and—yes—even great. They are dedicated to a cause, a mission in the truest sense of the word (as opposed to many bland "mission statements" that inspire nobody and stand for the ordinary and mundane).

Starbucks' commitment to creating a cafe ambience where people can forget their woes, Enron's commitment to forging ahead to help create a globally deregulated utility market, Swatch's commitment to creating "joy of life"—this is a lot more than simply selling coffee or gas or timepieces. When you posit your company's work as a shared crusade, you can attract and cultivate a community of roadrunner evangelists to carry it out, akin to what an industry veteran told journalist John McLaughlin about ESPN: "ESPN is staffed by very driven people who would fall on their sword for it. They really believe what they are doing is important. They have been successful because of that attitude." Roadrunners are suckers for causes.

From Ignorance to Wisdom . . .

Wile E. Coyote is not dumb; he's just ignorant! He doesn't have a low IQ, just a limited imagination—he has ingenuity, but no insight. His shortsightedness claims his opportunities for success; his ill-informed intelligence robs him of a chance to prevail. He is hemmed in by self-imposed boundaries because he reacts instead of reflects. He shoots from the hip when a more thoughtful approach would yield a better outcome.

Learning is the way roadrunners gain not only competence, but also the wisdom for adaptability. It is a roadrunner's wisdom that fosters the power to operate outside normal bounds while his competence promotes security and confidence. Building competence can involve gaining information about the organization. Roadrunners know the organization's long-range goals. Roadrunners know the competition and what they are thinking. Roadrunners take time on weekends to shop competitors and then share what they learned. They are ever anxious to learn about the "business of the business." They borrow trade magazines to learn about the industry. The more curiosity they demonstrate, the more they discover options. And the more they learn, the better equipped they are to make front-line decisions "like an owner." In contrast, the myopic ignorance of the coyote is self-destructive:

Wile E. Coyote stands on top of a ledge watching the Road Runner in the valley below approaching at great speed. He reaches into a box nearby labeled "Acme Dehydrated Boulders—Just add water." Pulling out one tiny pebble, he places it in the palm of his hand. Using an eyedropper, he adds one droplet of water and holds it above his head as he continues to watch the approaching bird. The pebble quickly expands to a huge boulder and crushes Wile E. on the top of the ledge.

Dick Orfalea, Executive VP of Kinko's Copiers, doesn't mince words. "Training," he says, "is a profit-driver." Not a "cost," not an "investment," but a direct predictor of profit. Why? Because while the cost of traditional capital is going down, the cost of human capital is going up. He ticks off his reasons: Interest rates have remained stable, war is a low probability, the government is unlikely to screw up the economy, and with more people saving and pumping income into 401(k)s and pension funds, there's lots of money out there looking for good ideas. So attaining low costs of traditional capital doesn't differentiate winners from losers anymore. Instead, for business success today—and even more so tomorrow—you need brains, imagination, and customer obsession. The only way to build up return on investment is to build up human capital. Hence, says Orfalea, "training is the name of the game" in business today. For everyone on staff, to be sure, but as he warns, don't ever shortchange the front line.

From Fear to Confidence . . .

Wile E. Coyote crawls out to the edge of the narrow overhang and pushes an anvil in front of him, attached to a balloon. He shoves the anvil off the edge, the balloon holds it up, and it floats along. The Road Runner is running down the road. When he runs onto a bridge, Wile E. pulls the string separating the balloon from the anvil, and the anvil drops. The Road Runner stops dead. The anvil hits the bridge right in front of him and goes straight through. It hits the electrical wires below, which slingshot it back up through the bridge, all the way over Wile E.'s head. The anvil falls, but not squarely on Wile E. It hits on the overhang behind Wile E., cutting that piece of ground off. Wile E. is still standing on the overhang not realizing he is about to fall. He wipes his brow, thankful that the anvil didn't fall on his head. Then he realizes he is plummeting . . . all the way down.

The Road Runner is blissful; Wile E. is anxious. The Road Runner is joyful; Wile E. is grim. Other words used to describe the Road Runner: *confident, gleeful, happy.* Wile E. is not only "stern," "melancholy," "morose." There is another crucial difference. The Road Runner is confident. Not arrogant, not egotistical, but confident in his capacity to respond innovatively to whatever the coyote throws at him (including dynamite). In contrast, the feeling driving the personality of Wile E. is fear. He is deep-down scared. Scared of missing a meal, scared of losing, scared of getting his pride stomped, scared of being made to look foolish by this scrawny desert bird. His actions are dominated by fear, costing him the freedom to respond creatively.

Tennis pro Andre Agassi, who goes alternatively through periods of brilliance and funk but is nevertheless recognized as one of the super players of this era, once explained how he raised his level of play from good to championship. When he played with a fear of losing, he said, he was much more apt to lose than when he went out on the court with his focus on winning. The fear of losing kept him cautious, inhibited, tentative, and unconfident. It's only when he broke through his internal boundaries, when he willed his mind-set to change, that his fortunes changed as well.

The first step in boundary bashing is to know that *permeable* means open, accessible, and porous. Most of us first learned that concept in high school biology when we studied

amoebas. Roadrunner organizations are not without structure or order. They thrive with purposeful structures . . . tools
that enable and facilitate. Permeable organizations promote
the capacity of people flowing in and out of temporary units
as needed in order to function in a high-performance
fashion.

The concept of permeability for leaders is as powerful as it
is for organizations. Permeable leaders do not have an "open
door" policy; they foster a "no door" environment. They are
easy to get to and easy to be with. They show an obvious disdain for the use of rank, protocol, position, or title in ways
that inhibit comfort, produce distance, or repress access.
They work hard at being porous, that is, not inflexible, rigid,
or fixed. They make requests, not demands; issue invitations,
not directives. They inspire enrollment in a mission through
their competence and commitment, not their supremacy.
They know authority is the last resort of the inept . . . and the
frustrated.

Permeability is the secret to organizational freedom. It enables energy to be released so it can be channeled and mo-
bilized—people do not hold back their best stuff out of fear
it will be stolen, credited inappropriately, or serve as the basis
for rebuke. Permeability is the welcome mat for teams to
gather and pool their talents, an invitation to talents; it
beckons for synergy and partnership to come inside and
flourish.

BIRDSEED

- Make it your personal goal to smash organizational boundaries to speed and innovation.
- Personally decorate your office with homemade/self-made stuff—posters, artwork, and so on. Requirements: Use balloons and crayons, and do it yourself.
- Ask yourself constantly: "Am I a living example of our mission?" Make sure your actions are consistent with your organization's mission or purpose.
- Make cross-disciplinary work the rule, not the exception, for everyone's job.
- Insist that outsiders be members of every project and meeting.
- Develop friends you don't understand, hobbies you know little about. Lionize people in your organization who, despite gallant efforts, fail in a fashion that helps others learn.
- Identify one thing each week that you know nothing about or you feel uncomfortable doing. Then learn about it or do it.
- Encourage forums for collective discussion of dysfunctional myths. Make the line "What is the worst thing that could happen to you if you went ahead and did it?" a constant test on the pros and cons of effective action.

Tail Feathers: A Roadrunner Outside the Box

If you had seen Lars-Birger Larsson's job description a few years ago, you'd think, "Oh, yeah, another government bureaucrat." In 1974, Lars was hired by the National Swedish Board for Technical Development (STU, its Swedish acronym) as a "promoter of innovation." STU saw itself as a policy-making think tank. It viewed Lars's position ("help" to high-tech start-ups) as nothing more than a research-oriented university-like box. Lars saw things differently.

Lars Larsson has a passionate vision of turning Sweden into a Silicon Valley–like hotbed of free market entrepreneurialism. This may sound like a radical idea, but remember that Sweden has only eight million citizens and a terrific infrastructure—not unlike the greater San Jose/San Francisco area. So Lars turned his middle-management staff position into a unique form of support for high-tech start-ups, often against the triple tides of Swedish quasi-socialistic tradition, government bias favoring the support of big, old-line industry, and STU's own hierarchical inertia. How did he do it?

Well, as they say, how do you eat an elephant? One bite at a time. From 1974 to 1980, on a modest budget of $5 million Swedish kronor (SKr, where 7 SKr=$1 U.S.), Lars launched seminars and conferences on topics like obtaining venture capital, creating a corporate culture of constant product innovation and customer service, and shifting government priorities to support start-up activities. These gatherings were both informative and controversial; they also provided a watering hole for like-minded individuals to meet one other and mobilize national action.

Lars was then ready to go further. In the 1980s, he lobbied for a bigger budget and got it—first 10 million, then 15 million SKr annually. He began to use the money to make direct-risk loans to promising companies on unconventional terms; if the start-up succeeded, the loan would be paid back with interest; if it failed, the loan would be forgiven. Lars's strategy was twofold: One, he wanted to establish a critical mass of Swedish start-ups that would be cutting-edge, first-to-market, world-class, export-driven players. Two, he wanted to shape a network of entrepreneurs who were committed to a new way of doing business in Sweden—a Silicon Valley way rather than a protectionist, controlled-economy way.

And so the Network evolved, a dynamic group of competent, successful entrepreneurs in young high-tech companies. By 1995, the Network had expanded to the point that Lars was dispensing 90 million SKr annually to new start-ups. A new grassroots force in Sweden, small but powerful, had emerged.

The national press took notice. A government investigation concluded with laudatory remarks. The pace of regional risk capital company start-ups quickened. Bridges for transferring knowledge from research to industry formed. The middle-manager government employee who preferred to stay in the background had instigated a subtle but unmistakable new momentum for change in Swedish business.

In 1996, Lars was wooed away from STU by the Stockholm-based venture capital firm SwedeStart. He worked with the firm for two years, regularly tapping into the Network and keeping in sharp focus his vision of a new Sweden, but this time as a senior manager with venture capital as a tool. In late 1998, Lars left SwedeStart and brought together government contacts at STU with local farmers and landowners in a rural region north of Stockholm to share in a $10 million SKr loan to start up an enterprise to produce specialty filters and antennas for the mobile phone industry. Yet another goal consistent with his vision of a high-tech, high-growth, twenty-first-century Sweden—and another step in expanding the Network.

If there is anyone who embodies the principles of "everyone a full player" and "breakthrough as the road to prosperity," Lars-Birger Larsson is that person. Oren recently asked him to summarize his two-decade experience as a government employee in a job that many would have found purely academic or highly restrictive. As he reflected on his time at STU, he noted that he and his colleagues investigated over 3,000 start-up ideas, provided 500 projects with financial support, financed 200 small young high-tech companies (primarily in mobile telephony, electronics, optics, and computer products), conducted 180 large seminars on themes central to those companies' interests, and consciously created a unique, open, symbiotic, supportive network of inventors, entrepreneurs, and researchers across Sweden.

Yes, Lars can also easily recount his investment failures, but he points out that "usually the failures were fast, so not much money was lost." On the other hand, from 1980 to 1995, the revenue base of the Network doubled every second year; in 1998 the revenue base of its 200 member companies was 10 billion SKr, a fine return on the 200 million SKr initially invested. Many of these companies continue to thrive as private enterprises, some have successfully gone public, others have been bought out by larger firms.

And how would he sum it all up? Lars's response, as usual, was succinct: "I had a very interesting job. I did what I wanted. I had a great purpose." Understated, powerful, spoken like a true roadrunner.

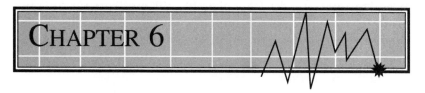

CHAPTER 6

Fleeting
All Enterprise Is Virtual

In 1996, there appeared a host of TV infomercials touting a new, exciting exercise product that promised to tone up your abs. The device was almost ridiculously simple, just a metal frame that gave you head and arm support while you did sit-ups to firm your abdominal muscles. You still see them today in gyms and fitness centers. They're also in many private homes, and therein lies the story.

Maybe you remember the endless stream of celebrity ads and endorsements. There was a point when you could channel-surf on cable and see competing infomercials broadcasting simultaneously, each hawking its own version of this little contraption. The frenzy went on for months and then abruptly ceased. What happened to this hot fad that suddenly went cold?

Originally, a few people conceived the device and realized that once sales got rolling the marginal cost of production would be near zero. They registered themselves as companies, subcontracted practically every function—including manufacturing, administration, and distribution—and proceeded to do what they did best: marketing the heck out of the abs apparatus, primarily through television. With this business model—"an asset-less" organization to the nth degree—it was clear that barriers to entry were negligible. So other people got into the act with their own "companies," and competing abs devices, all simple variations of the same product, proliferated.

These products sold and sold and sold! In fact, the "industry" sold a *half-billion dollars'* worth until the word got out through ABC's *20/20* and NBC's *Dateline* that you could condition your abs just as well by doing free sit-ups with your legs resting on any raised platform, like a chair. At this point, the entire industry disappeared.

There were no corporate properties to close, no fixed costs to liquidate, no payroll to downsize, since none of these had existed in the first place. Some of the original companies immediately went on to pitch new products for different parts of the body. The abs product is still a commodity for mainstream retailers like Sears and Oshman's. But the heyday of the high-profile, lucrative abs industry was over.

This story is a foreshadowing of the future. Not that the future holds legions of hollow organizations or "Scams R Us," but rather that the hallmark of successful business on the horizon will be their virtual nature and processes that can turn on a dime. In a 1995 summit at the Massachusetts Institute of Technology, one participant described the post-2000 business environment as "a world in which there are many, many firms with only one person, and many others with fewer than fifteen people. These firms would come together in temporary combinations for various projects. Work is already organized like this for producing movies, organizing conventions, and constructing large buildings." So, the message from the abs machine industry is this: Find a great idea, patch together a group of disparate players with a common goal, and work frenetically together to create and deliver something unique to a clearly defined market. Then, just as quickly, disband when the market is saturated and go on to something else.

Roadrunners Have Connections

All enterprise is becoming virtual. Organizations harness each other's strengths via alliances, subcontracts, partnerships, and co-contracts to become fast, focused, and—just as important—fleeting. Tom Peters describes the emerging marketplace as one populated by "ephemeral 'organizations' joined in ephemeral combinations to produce ephemeral products for ephemeral markets . . . FAST."

Whether you're dealing with financial services, advertising, construction, consumer products, manufacturing, or exercise equipment, the last thing you want is to be bolted down with the weight of debt, corporate mass, and routine, peddling a tired, same-old-same-old product or service. Thriving in the emerging economy will require being light, agile, and magical. When you do it well, your product line, niche strategy, or entire organization can literally disappear and reappear in response to market forces, just like that . . . just like the Road Runner!

Ever notice that in the cartoons, the Road Runner frequently appears—and disappears—as a blur or a puff of dust? He's never a clear target. He's never in one spot and never the same. He has no anchors, no routines, no predictability. He strikes no stationary poses for easy viewing (and easy capturing) by Wile E. Coyote. You can't pin the Road Runner down. By contrast, once Wile E. concocts one of his very elaborate schemes, based on very reasonable predictions about where and when the Road Runner will show up, he sticks with it—he's static. And he is invariably wrong!

111

The Road Runner is dashing across the desert being chased by Wile E., who has his arms outstretched, tongue wagging out. Wile E. comes to a three-way fork in the road. He can't see the Road Runner anymore. All he sees are dust trails down all three paths. He stops and scratches his head. The Road Runner suddenly appears behind Wile E. and Beeps. Wile E. leaps straight up in shock and then crashes down on his rear, while the Road Runner zooms off. Now angry, Wile E. hunches his shoulders, clenches his fists, and turns around to see where the Road Runner went. Again, the Road Runner materializes behind him, "Beep Beeps," and takes off. Wile E. chases him and eventually winds up going over the edge of the cliff. The camera cuts to the bottom of the cliff, where we see Wile E. scratching his head in puzzlement.

Each Road Runner–Wile E. Coyote scene tells the same story: An aggressive, obsessive coyote is attempting to capture an ephemeral, will-o'-the-wisp roadrunner. Constant frustration. However, the Coyote's frustration is not simply that the Road Runner seems to run faster. What he doesn't understand is how the Road Runner can be in one place one moment, then reappear in a completely different place; how he can be in plain sight one second, a puff of air the next. Wile E. is portrayed as continuously baffled and confused by his "virtual target." The first scene in these cartoons invariably has Wile E. giving up the chase temporarily, narrowing his eyes, scratching some part of his anatomy, and starting to hatch an elaborate scheme. The scheme is developed and executed in the subsequent scene, and that's what begins the fray that, as spectators, we've come to love.

Wile E. Coyote is waiting behind a sign by the side of the road. As the Road Runner goes by, Wile E. jumps out and starts chasing. The Road Runner stops cold and turns to run in the opposite direction. Wile E. doesn't and promptly gets flattened by an oncoming truck. The action resumes with the Road Runner running at full speed, with Wile E. giving chase, his arms flailing. The Road Runner makes a sharp left turn, then another left, then another—leaving trailing dust behind him indicating perfect right angles. Wile E. keeps running, turns his head around, then his body, then finally stops his legs, looking puzzled. He turns around, and there's the Road Runner in front of him. The Road Runner "Beep Beeps," leaps into the air, does a 180 degree turn, and roars off. Wile E.—eyes wide, ears drooping—holds up a sign saying "EGAD," then another sign "!!!" He then drops the signs and scratches his chin, as if coming up with a plan.

Roadrunner companies follow the adage: Nothing's for long, nothing's permanent, nothing lasts. "Long"—as in long lead times, long production runs, and long product life cycles—is a remnant of a bygone era. Smart companies like Hewlett-Packard and Quad/Graphics cannibalize, abandon, and then reinvent successful products before someone else does. Fat cash cows in any business are on the fast train to extinction. Today's competitors tell us nothing about what tomorrow's competitors will be like, or even *who* they'll be. Long-term strategic planning these days is defined in terms of months, not years.

The CEO of a small firm that designs and manufactures gold bracelets, necklaces, and other jewelry for "big box" retailers like Wal-Mart and Target told us: "It used to be that if I had a great concept and could get it out to market quickly, I'd have an eighteen- to twenty-four-month grace period. Now, I'm lucky if I have three months." A couple of years ago Bill Gates probably felt the same. Bill Gates? The richest guy in the world? The chairman of the company that inspires awe, fear, and/or loathing? Yes, indeed.

When Gates finally "got it"—that a wide-open Web and free browsers to navigate it threatened to topple the monolith that Microsoft had become (the same way new market forces had already toppled so many once-mighty Fortune 500 companies)—he acted with alacrity. In a state of extreme urgency, he engineered one of the biggest corporate reversals in recent business history. And in a matter of a few months he had guided Microsoft's transformation from its operating-system-and-software-package roots into an Internet-based company, replete with Web products as diverse as browsers, money management tools, encyclopedias, travel services, and games. In response to an unknown tiny upstart like Netscape, even a dominant company like Microsoft came to the startling realization that successful corporate strategy is a fleeting reality.

Market realities appear and disappear; so does good strategy. Even if that strategy catapulted you to success in the past, you have to make it disappear when the marketplace changes, or else *you* disappear. Just look at semidefunct companies like Smith-Corona and Singer for verification. Nowadays, the grace period for strategies is shrinking, which means that the tempo for abandoning today's strategy is picking up. Witness, for example, the ever-intensifying convulsions faced by companies in the telecommunications industry—which leads us to the next point.

Words like *fleeting* and *virtual* aren't limited to products and companies; they describe entire industries. In 1997, the telecommunications world turned upside down in a matter of four months, during which time the staid orderly marriage arrangements between British Telecom and MCI were upended by the entry of Jackson, Mississippi, based WorldCom.

The $37 billion deal that ensued cemented the rapid transition of telecommunications from a voice-transmission industry to one where the significant players will be able to deliver customized, global, often-wireless bundles of voice, video, and data through new, high-speed, high-bandwidth pipelines. Accordingly, a whole slew of new roadrunner upstarts are joining WorldCom in creating this new world of telecom . . . companies like WinStar, Qwest, Level 3, Williams Communications, and Lucent Technologies.

Nothing is fixed, stable, or static anymore—not even pricing. The Internet and every other means of electronic and wireless networking means that buyers and sellers are more directly connected to each other than ever before—so it's easy to make constant price adjustments and do electronic horse trading. The new technologies allow a constant stream of real-time fluctuations of prices to be accessed and acted upon by anyone—just like ESPN SportsZone or E*Trade lists changes in sports scores and stock scores, respectively, up to thousands of times per hour.

The amalgam of search engines (like Yahoo! or Excite!), "bots" (software robots like Junglee or Agentsoft that act as personal search agents in cyberspace), and the Web sites of Internet companies like eBay, Priceline.com, and Buy.com are the precursors of a new model of business: You the consumer name the product or service you want (like a consumer good, an airline ticket, an insurance policy, a mortgage loan) and state the terms and conditions you wish (including what you're willing to pay), and we'll figure out how to match your needs with what's out there at any given point of time. Try us in ten minutes, and we may have a better deal for you.

eBay offers a powerful peephole into the future. The symbolic importance of eBay is not simply that it is an internet auction house. It is that buyers and sellers of anything can now be connected with one another instantaneously. In the emerging digital economy, the capacity to provide direct unfiltered one-to-one communication with anyone changes the entire landscape of business. The Internet now allows direct conversation, no filters, no barriers. A lot of what goes on in organizations is about barriers to direct connection (functional, vertical, bureaucratic policies and procedures, arm's-length walls with outside constituencies). Companies have to catch up with the technology because the technology now allows anyone (especially roadrunners, who'll jump on this technology) to connect with one another. What eBay does is show that even among people who don't know one another and live thousands of miles from one another, there is now a capacity to allow direct conversation.

How far can it go? The following item went up for bid on the eBay Web site: "Team of 16 employees from major ISP (Internet Service Provider) willing to leave as a group. Group formed major ISP presence in Silicon Valley/USA and is now looking for other challenges and requires an opportunity with a major player." Since each eBay auction item requires an asking price, this was no different: The asking price was $3.14 million. This included salaries (generally in the $100,000–$200,000 range), as well as a signing bonus and stock options. Roadrunner employees can now—individually or as a team—walk away from your coyote organization and get hired by a competitor via the medium of the Internet.

This is the world of the roadrunner: fluid, dynamic, ever-changing—requiring alert anticipation, fast thinking, quick action, immediate response. Internet companies like DoubleClick and SmartAge are seeking ways of brokering ads and banners on the Internet—ads and banners that are in constant motion. The San Francisco–based SmartAge, for example, has created a new technology Smart Clicks, which tracks which ads are going where and which ones people click. It then automatically routes its client companies' ads to similar sites. The technology allows ads to appear where they are most likely to be seen, with automatic, constant updates. As a result, SmartAge ads are clicked on 1.8 to 2.4 percent of the time, compared to an industry standard of 0.6 to 0.9 percent in the rest of the Web.

Here one moment, gone the next—that's how the Road Runner thrives. Here today, gone tomorrow—that's how good businesses thrive in any industry. All enterprise is virtual.

Nothing is forever. It's a tough lesson. The old model of enterprise, the one with which we're most comfortable, is based on the appearance—if not the fact—of permanence, of substance, of place, suppliers, employees, customers, market conditions, products, corporate processes, and structures. Our organizations and management thinking are built for stability and order. We get our ducks in a row, our processes in place, our job descriptions clarified, our functional fiefdoms and caste system hierarchies installed, and our suppliers and distributors enrolled with reams of legal documentation. We focus on improving cost efficiencies, reducing waste, maximizing synergies, and optimizing economies of scale in our existing routines. It's all very sensible . . . until the Road Runner comes along and teaches us that our approach is slow, cumbersome, needlessly complex, and dated.

Wile E. Coyote is lying on his belly at the edge of a cliff, looking down on the road below. He's holding a big metal bucket. When the Road Runner runs past, Wile E. throws the bucket onto the bird and appears to trap him. He immediately jumps down, lands on top of the upside-down bucket, pulls out a stick of dynamite, lights it, lifts the edge of the bucket up just enough to slide the dynamite underneath, and then lies on the bucket with a victorious smile. Just then the Road Runner runs up to Wile E. Wile E. is shocked, looks down at the bucket, looks back at the Road Runner, who sticks out his tongue, makes a puckering noise, and runs off. At this point things begin to degenerate predictably. Wile E. looks at us in the audience (as if to say, "What's going on?"), lifts up the edge of the bucket a little, then a little more, and crawls in to search, until he himself is under the bucket. He stands up with the bucket balancing on his head, forgetting that the dynamite is now lying at his feet. Need we go on?

In every cartoon, Wile E.'s behavior follows a predictable routine. We have seen his strategic plan and know what Wile E.'s new gleaming Acme steamroller is supposed to do. We also know that something will go awry big-time. And as Wile E. is chasing the runaway steamroller up the hill, we know the force of gravity will eventually cause the steamroller to come back down and flatten him. And, of course, it does.

Roadrunners Are Seasonal Birds

Preoccupation with permanence and predictability can ultimately lead to death—no matter how efficiently or "synergistically" it is done. The fashion industry understands this better than most. Clearly, people in fashion have to achieve production cost efficiencies and pursue economies of scale in their global purchasing. But they also realize that that alone is no prescription for success.

If you're Calvin Klein, The Limited, Yves St. Laurent, or Paloma Picasso, you know in your bones that thriving long term depends on your products being ephemeral. You don't *want* them to last. Your fantasy is that even as your customers are thrilled with your products today, they will be salivating for your next wave of entirely new designs tomorrow, which you're feverishly working on right now. You do not live five years to five years or fiscal year to fiscal year. You live season to season, and the seasons are getting shorter and shorter!

Fashion people know that fickle, impatient customers served by hyper-obsessed, hyper-creative competitors in a volatile, whitewater-like environment are not the downside of their business—these are the givens of their business. And, if they're smart, they know these givens drive the business—they stimulate excitement and creativity—and the big winners capitalize on them. These factors force winners in the fashion business to be virtual in what they do, how they do it, and what market offerings they ultimately present.

And now, as Tom Peters and McKinsey's Kenichi Ohmae

have noted, we are *all* in the fashion business! Fashion market realities (fickle impatient customers) are the realities every business is increasingly facing. Roadrunners are capitalizing on these realities in the same way the fashion moguls do. Roadrunners think "seasonal," not "everlasting."

The most successful companies now "fashionize" their products and services to differentiate themselves from dull commodities. Think about what Nike has done to the simple "sneaker," what Sony has done to the "radio," what Ritz-Carlton has done to the "inn," what ESPN has done to "sports reporting," what Schwab has done to "investing." They've turned commodities into pure fashion—exciting options, dazzling presentations, cool designs, outrageous quality, extraordinary meshing with customer's conscious and subconscious needs. When we talk to Jim Thompson—who's turning Houston-based Vallen Corporation from a purveyor of commodity safety equipment (eye goggles, gloves) to a purveyor of customized safety solutions, or when we read about a new product called Power Worms, which are fishing lures with a tiny computer chip built inside to simulate real bait—we know successful players in every industry are entering the ephemeral world of fads, fashion, and fancies.

Roadrunners Blend with a Changing Environment

"But wait!" you argue. If fashion means ephemeral, seasonal, fleeting, virtual—how do you explain the customer who is attracted to the "permanence" of Sony product quality, the "predictability" of Ritz-Carlton responsiveness, or the "stability" of cool Nike technology and design?

Customers *know* what they're getting when they deal with any brand—be it Calvin Klein, Disney, Nordstrom, Dell Computer, or Kinko's. But their attraction to the brand name is not the desire to buy a routine, unchanging product or service. The value they count on is the reassurance that they are buying the most cutting-edge, most snazzy, most appropriate, and, increasingly, most customized package for their individual needs. In other words, they are after something that is constantly changing for the better.

James Collins and Jerry Porras note in their bestseller *Built to Last* that the companies that have prospered the longest are those who "preserve the core" (core skills, core values) while they "stimulate progress." They are ever watchful of a changing marketplace environment and blend with its flow . . . while retaining their unique grounding. Whether you're an investor or a customer, you sleep better knowing that the Dayton Hudson or Pfizer or Schwab market offerings are perpetually evolving, growing, becoming ever more customer responsive—*they are never staying the same.*

Brandeis University professor and former Secretary of Labor Robert Reich puts it well when he says that customers "don't just want assurance they're getting what they used to get. They want a trusted guide to what's new." Accordingly, he says, winning companies "stand not for specific products, but for continuing solutions." Disney not only continually buffs up and adds to its core theme parks (like the $1 billion Animal Park built with tons of customer input), but also grows its platter of market offerings by giving people fresh options and tools to enhance their experience of entertainment. As we noted earlier, a new Disney product (game, video, toy, movie) pops into the marketplace every five minutes. It's an all-organic modus operandi, with the various bits metamorphosing, appearing, and disappearing when no longer viable. All Disney enterprise is virtual.

Roadrunners Have Eagle Eyes

Another hallmark of today's roadrunner virtual enterprises is their focus on the market of one, the individual customer. A vendor who is sincerely committed to market units of one must by definition be virtual, for each customer (their needs, wants, concerns, expectations, and partnership capabilities) is perpetually changing. Unisys Corporation is not known as a high-flyer stock. The company has suffered some serious challenges, which to its credit it is steadily overcoming. Within that environment has arisen a roadrunner division headed by Jim McGuirk. It's the Federal Systems unit, which deals with the supposedly unglamorous and ultra-cost-conscious government and public sector market, yet from 1996 to 1998 enjoyed an average growth rate of around 30 percent (industry growth average in that niche: 4 percent) and exceeded a billion dollars in revenues in 1998 (in 1995 McGuirk predicted he'd hit $1 billion by year 2000, a goal even Unisys insiders thought impossible). What McGuirk did in 1995 was to change the division's mission: Federal Systems would no longer be a provider of mainframes but a provider of integrated technology services, including telecommunications and network integration, data center consolidation, Y2K interventions, information systems engineering, software applications, and facilities management. As part of this equation, Federal Systems now sells nonmainframe as well as mainframe hardware—*including competitors' products.* Whatever the individual customer—the market of one—needs.

Accordingly, Federal Systems embeds itself with each of its clients, customizing its efforts entirely, and growing the scope of these efforts (along with its revenues and margins) as it grows the relationship. Its business model is predicated on the assumption that the customer of the future (aka today) does not want a "product" or "service." The customer wants a provider who understands his constantly changing business and can quickly respond, even anticipate, her constantly changing needs—and provide unique value right away.

For example, Federal Systems has helped the Internal Revenue Service by supplying a steady stream of new approaches to network integration that continue to reduce cycle times and cost sharply. As part of this process, since the IRS already owned a large number of IBM and Unisys machines, Unisys didn't try to sell them on the idea of dumping those machines and replacing them with Unisys substitutes or updates. Instead, with the active participation of IRS experts (open dialogue, sharing of data—same old story), Unisys developed a comprehensive system which integrated IBM hardware and appropriate Unisys tools to address most effectively unique IRS concerns. The Unisys plan even called for purchasing some new IBM equipment. Unisys went on to earn a lucrative twelve-year contract with the IRS—very unusual among public sector organizations—because the IRS became positively *addicted* to the way their vendor does business.

As a result of these market-of-one approaches with its clients, Federal Systems constantly winds up redefining and reinventing its own business—new competencies, new services, new products, new networks, new possibilities emerge as the division flows and grows with each of its customers. It's a roadrunner business model if we ever saw one, one that changes shape, evolves, becomes virtual as the division learns and adapts with each customer.

The Virtual Way

The value of a virtual company does not come from its products or services, but from its knowledge, its web of alliances, and its capacity to transform know-how into results. Roadrunner organizations succeed on their ability to form and unform as customer preferences and the marketplace environment changes.

As the environment changes, so does the roadrunner's way of living. Levi Strauss's capacity to create custom-built Original Spin jeans is only the first step. The customer tries on a sample pair of prototype jeans and her geometry is beamed directly to a facility where the jeans are made to order robotically. The next step, presumably, is to improve and expand the process to cover all Levi's products (not just women's jeans, as it is now) and all Levi's retail outlets (not just at twenty-five Original Levi's stores). Then what? The next step could be developing—perhaps in alliance with a technology firm—a way for customers to provide the necessary data through a Web interaction from the comfort of home. The next step would be to provide customers with the means to literally design their own clothing from an electronic interactive catalog, with help from Levi's consultants, again from the comfort of their home. Perhaps the next step is to apply this model to other consumer goods, from camping gear to athletic goods. The next step would be . . . WHO KNOWS? The logical extension is to redefine the entire world of retailing the way, say, Dell is reinventing the world of computer manufacturing, distribution, and sales. Doing it the road-runner way. Nothing stays put. Nothing lasts. All enterprise is virtual.

John McElroy, editor of *Automotive Industries,* says: "There's really the capability, today, to form a virtual car company. You can go to independent design firms, like Porsche Engineering, which can design an entire car from roof to road, and bumper to bumper. There are suppliers out there that can build every single part, and component, and module that goes into making a car. And now there are even several supplier companies out there with the capability of assembling vehicles. It's only a matter of time before someone comes along and puts these together on sort of a cooperative basis. In other words, you don't have to go out and buy and own all this stuff. You can go out and form a virtual company." If this is true for cars, it's true for any industry.

So what does it all mean for you? Beware of anything that bogs you down, that unnecessarily ties you to a particular locale or niche—be it a strategic plan, product line, fixed asset, real estate, or well-honed habits. Beware of allegiance to any physical inanimate object, like a permanent office, tangible location, a corporate headquarters campus, any hardware or system. Beware of allegiance to "we've always done it this way," regardless of whether that statement applies to your strategy, products, personnel, service delivery, relations with suppliers and partners, or corporate culture. Be leery of "tradition."

Seek the path that is perpetually virtual, changing, mysterious, fleeting. Stay light of foot—carry a knapsack instead of bulging suitcases. Understand that there's no such thing as "my" department, "my" people, or "my" budget. Whether you're first-level supervisor or a COO, you are a steward of assets for a fleeting moment.

"When your product gets obsolete," advised Polaroid founder Edwin Land, "make sure you're the one who obsoletes it." Or as a Japanese executive we know put it: "The quicker we can abandon today's successful product, the stronger and more profitable we'll be." In the fashion world, the only sure thing is that whatever you are doing is going to be obsolete pretty soon, so the only really interesting question is: Who's going to do the obsoleting? Start viewing your organization, your product line, and your career as *experiments.* In his book *Leapfrogging the Competition,* Oren describes a "no sacred cow" culture as one which "treats everything that is currently done (plans, products, policies, processes, structures, methods, meeting agenda, etc.) as an experiment. This means that everything is open to challenge, testing and renewal."

Never allow yourself to get bolted to the ground. Appear anywhere; ally with great players anywhere. The Road Runner both uses and is part of the desert in the same spirit. He doesn't "own" the desert. He doesn't have a permanent address he takes seriously. There's no roadrunner birdhouse with a picket fence and a mailbox for Wile E. to deposit dynamite. If you are a fleeting player, ready to capitalize on an unpredictable ever-enduring marketplace, you thrive.

Wile E. is sitting on a rock reading a book entitled *Western Cookery*. He's salivating at a page showing a picture of a roadrunner, with the text reading: "Possibly the most delicious of all Western Game Birds is the Road Runner." He turns to the next page: "Road Runner Surprise: Secure one (1) Road Runner, baste in slow oven. . . ." Wile E. smiles and licks his lips. The Road Runner quietly runs up right behind him, looks over his shoulder at the cookbook, and licks his lips (that is, beak) too. Wile E. turns around; the Road Runner "Beep Beeps" in his face, sending Wile E. shooting through the air in shock, the force causing his head to bore right through an overhanging cliff.

The Roadrunner Leader in a Virtual Enterprise

As enterprises become increasingly virtual, people in alliances and partnerships will increasingly need to enterprise. *Enterprise* (the verb) is cut from the same cloth as the new term *to office*. To enterprise means to locate and integrate opportunities, ventures, alliances, and resources. In the virtual, real-time world, the line between our personal and professional lives will blur. To enterprise will also include finding good balance so capacities remain fresh and honed, not burned out or dull.

Roadrunner leaders in a virtual enterprise are unmoved by factors that have no impact on continuous and evolving performance—gender, color, age, style, tradition, economic status. They are egalitarian and entrepreneurial. Such a leader spends time nurturing relationships that have the potential for synergy down the road. They link people who are not normally linked. They bring together disparate resources with cooperative potential. They value the unique, the odd, and the zany and believe that diversity brings richness, depth, and artistry to any endeavor. Roadrunners encourage potential and know how to summon unknown, unrealized, or unrecognized talents and gifts from those they influence. They are slow to critique and quick to affirm.

Roadrunner leaders help keep the vision or goal perpetually in the thoughts of those they work with. They remind people of their collective purpose, keeping them anchored to a calling grander than simply doing the task. They know that, while vision without performance is daydreaming, action without vision is aimless activity. They tell stories of vision-aligned heroics, especially about behind-the-scenes heroes. And they are diligent and disciplined in constantly modeling purposeful zeal. When former Herman Miller CEO Max De Pree said in *Leadership Is an Art* that "The first job of a leader is to create reality, the last job is to say 'thank you.' Everything in between is serving associates," he had roadrunner leaders in mind.

What's the overarching goal? To do anything to lighten the drag, shrug off the yokes, make yourself lighter and more ephemeral so that your competitors will see you the way Wile E. sees the Road Runner . . . as a transitory blur, disappearing now, appearing anywhere the next moment! Completely unpredictable to the observer, but always at one with your marketplace, your environment.

BEEP! BEEP!

BIRDSEED

- Don't be afraid to enter any niche where your core skills can take you.
- Appear anywhere. Seek customers, partners, employees, distributors, suppliers anywhere on the planet.
- Eliminate (sell, outsource, give up) all fixed tangible assets, personnel, and functions that do not directly reflect your strategic strengths.
- Encourage a culture of "everything as experiment" and "creative abandonment": Ask departments to describe how they would make themselves obsolete in response to market opportunities. Then insist they do it and reinvent themselves.
- Encourage people to alter their jobs and functions perpetually in order to create new value; encourage constant experimentation with internal processes and external product/service mixes.
- Strip away bulgy corporate staffs, prune down management levels, get rid of all that weight that keeps organizations slow, bolted down, and utterly vanilla-tepid in their responses. Eliminate fixed anything—job descriptions, functions, lines of authority. Insist that everyone continually re-create their jobs by choosing to work in temporary, ad hoc, cross-disciplinary teams.
- Work and dress casually, in every sense of the word.
- Provide people with a laptop, a cell phone, training, and accountability, and tell them to meet and organize themselves anywhere they need to in order to add value and agility to what they're doing now.

Tail Feathers: A Roadrunner As Virtual Virtuoso

Forbes magazine acclaimed her a "one-woman rooting section for would-be do-it-yourself entrepreneurs." Tomima Edmark is an entrepreneur's entrepreneur—an inventor of countless products and an innovator of cutting-edge business management practices. Her Dallas-based company, TopsyTail, started in 1989, has only a handful of employees, yet rings up hundreds of millions of dollars in sales.

TopsyTail sells to young women unique hair accessories, jewelry, dolls, you name it—whatever new products Tomima can invent. She is also a regular columnist for *Entrepreneur* magazine, the author of several books, and the winner of countless honors, as well as a guest on *Good Morning America, Dateline, 20/20*, and *Oprah*. She currently is launching an array of products focused on kissing, including a kissing machine. And, at forty, she is just warming up! Tomima is pure roadrunner.

How does she do it? One key is her deep appreciation for the power of the virtual enterprise. "I don't know if I'm a very good manager of employees," she says, "but I think I am a *very* good manager of vendors. That's why I use outsourcing so much. We outsource almost everything—HR, customer service, manufacturing, advertising, distribution. The one exception is information. Information is the most valuable asset a company has."

Tomima thinks outsourcing is a "fabulous" way to get things done, especially for her company. The advantages as she sees them? "I can buy instant expertise. I don't have to go out and hire employees and deal with a learning curve. I also don't have to fire them when they're done!"

Another advantage of Tomima's virtual business design is that outsourcing frees her to focus on her target customers. And she's more than willing and able to get up close and personal.

> I'm very hands-on. I do a lot of the work myself. People are sometimes surprised that I haven't delegated certain duties to people. But again, I think that's a part of staying suc-

cessful. You've got to keep your hand on the pulse of the consumer. For instance, the HALO, which we're trying to market, is doing extremely well. I pick up the 800 number when it rings just as much as our answering service or other people in the office. And I take orders and nobody has a clue that it is me. I want to hear what the customer is asking, what the issues are . . . it just really keeps me in touch.

Understand the power of outsourcing, and stay tuned in to your customers' changing needs—these are the touchstones of Tomima's success. So what other advice would Tomima give young leaders who aspire to be roadrunners?

First, have a dream. Then, figure out if there is a market for your dream. Even if you are presently an employee. And never underestimate the value of your naïveté! When I look back on some of the things I did, they were gross business mistakes. But I didn't know it at the time. Consequently I got information that I wouldn't have gotten otherwise because I think the person was so flabbergasted by my question—that I was so naive or dumb—that they just gave me stuff, thinking, "We'll give her the information because she's going nowhere."

Of course she did go somewhere . . . and built an exemplary roadrunner-era business, one that's long on imagination and short on old business mind-sets like traditional notions of top-down leadership. "You know, I'm not sure we're going to have leaders in the business world in the future," she says. "I mean, people like Bill Gates [a childhood playmate of hers] or a president of a company."

I really see in the business world there's going to be a lot of onesy, twosy people out there. With faxes and the Internet and the ability to not have to go to work, people are becoming their own little company . . . so I really don't see leadership per se growing. If anything I see it diminishing.

129

And I don't think leaders are going to be people that we look up to as much as people who did some gut success and did it in a very clever way. People are going to want to mimic that.

Very roadrunner!

CHAPTER 7

Character
Honorable Cultures Are Powerful

Wile E. Coyote and the Road Runner are but two adversaries in the eternal struggle of light vs. dark. Their creator, Chuck Jones, didn't set out to have the dueling duo personify an existential conflict between polar forces—he simply wanted a comic contest. "The Road Runner never defeats Wile E.," says Chuck Jones. "He's just amused at all the ways Wile E. defeats himself."

Nevertheless, part of their allure is the same tension that left us cheering Luke Skywalker in his duel with Darth Vader. In life, a coyote is the epitome of venal corruption; he's

both predator and scavenger, feeding on the bodies of animals that have died from injury, illness, or old age, or that have been killed by other animals. In that sense, the Road

Runner could join that long list of heroes with names like Rocky, Roy Rogers, and Rin Tin Tin.

We want to believe that humankind—like the Road Runner—is basically good. We want to believe that innocence and imagination will defeat deviousness and malice. While we know that most of us embody bits of both characters, we hope that most often the Road Runner side of our character dominates.

Wile E. posts a road sign: "STOP Free Birdseed." Naturally, the speeding Road Runner stops and starts pecking at the birdseed. On the ledge above, Wile E. points a cannon straight at the unsuspecting bird and lights the fuse. True to form, the cannon slips out of its holder and starts to fall with Wile E. on top. You know the ending. The Road Runner finishes the birdseed and departs the scene just as Wile E. gets smashed by the cannon.

Pop Quiz: Are You a Coyote or a Roadrunner?

The Road Runner is consistently noble. While he possesses an impish charm from time to time, he never deviates from his core style of dealing with the greedy Coyote in ways which are noncombative and uncorrupted. Examine your actions and motives and consider: Are you more like the Road Runner or the Coyote? The following seven mini-scenarios are about character—simple and complex issues we've all faced or easily could. Read and answer each one quickly. Be candid. No one is looking!

- Have you ever told your boss (or partner or associate) a lie?
- Have you ever deceived an employee, customer, supplier, or partner?
- Have you ever intentionally withheld information that would reflect negatively on you?
- Have you ever set up a colleague for failure?
- If your children observed your actions at work (assume you have children if you do not), what conclusions would they draw about your ethics? What lessons would they learn?
- Reflect on the last deal, negotiation, or conflict you had. What would your opponent or adversary conclude about your core values?
- If a naive observer looked at your daily calendar, your daily behavior, and your daily decisions—could they easily infer what you stand for?

"So, what's the point?" you may ask. "We aren't immoral or unethical, and we sure don't want anyone to think of us that way, but why would anyone want a work setting populated with super-honorable people? It's the real world out there. Aren't we better off with employees who are driven to win at any price, to end always on their feet no matter if someone is under them when they land? What can we gain by insisting on soft, squishy concepts like honor?

Wile E. Coyote is not an immoral or unethical character. Yet, we would never call Wile E. "honorable." He seeks to get what he wants without much thought of the consequences. Some might call him ruthless (as in "without ruth" or mercy . . . à la the biblical Ruth).

A blueprint reading, "Do it Yourself Exploding Camera Kit. Fool Your Friends. Be Popular!" shows an old-time camera with a gun attached. Wile E. sets up the camera and gets behind it, pulling the black drapery over his head. On the road is a sign: "Stop. Free Snapshots. Road Runners Only!" An arrow points to Wile E. The Road Runner runs up to the sign, reads it, runs to the camera, and Beeps. Wile E. pulls the trigger and the gun backfires. The Road Runner sticks out his tongue, says "Beep Beep," and runs off. Wile E., his head smoking from the blast, walks to the front of the camera and slowly unscrews the lens cover he forgot to remove.

In scene after scene we observe Wile E. attempt to ensnare the Road Runner . . . one time by offering free birdseed, another by promising free snapshots. Nothing illegal or even unethical about it, but certainly the shady way to confront his prey. In all cases Wile E. gets caught in his own deception . . . and the Road Runner emerges unscathed. The by-product of our own less-than-honorable actions is the same—we may prevail in the short run, but sooner or later we lose—it all blows up in our face.

Recall our earlier drill. Who is bigger, the Road Runner or Wile E. Coyote? The answer is obviously Wile E. Coyote. Who's physically stronger? Answer: Wile E. Who has the killer tools? Answer Wile E. Who has the muscle and resources of an ally like Acme? Answer: Wile E. Who has carefully developed attack and entrapment plans? Answer: Wile E. Who uses surprise and stealth? Answer: Wile E. Final question. Who *always* wins? The Road Runner!

What makes the Road Runner so successful? The Road Runner never resorts to trickery or deceit. He acts honorably. He operates with a consistency of spirit. Just as he has a full awareness of his environment, he has a full awareness of self. This operating-from-the-core confidence gives him much more power.

The Road Runner Is Pure Power

The word *power* has many meanings and connotations. In the military world, it means strength. In the utility world, it means energy. In the optics world, it means making things bigger and clearer. In the mathematics world, it is about multiplying something by itself to the nth degree. Roadrunner power has components of all of these. Wile E. can have all the stealth and strategic plans in the world, but the pulsing fluidity of the Road Runner power is stronger, bigger, and clearer—and its accelerating velocity means that as power, it increases exponentially out in the field.

His noncombative judo stance in the world proves to be stronger, more energetic, clear, and it multiplies . . . power propagates power. But, fundamentally, the Road Runner way connotes honor. The Road Runner is aerodynamically and tactically pure. He moves almost above the ground . . . at air speed, not at Wile E. dust-making, drag-laden, desperation-in-motion speed. And the Road Runner's honor enables him to be unstoppable . . . even when running through glue, a minefield, or quick-drying cement.

But what does this mean beyond the desert scene, in the less rarefied atmosphere of global business in the new millennium? What does a leader or organization gain by being honorable, by functioning from principle rather than utility or graft? Consider these benefits:

No Time Wasted Checking Stuff Out

Being honorable gives you agility and focus. Your energy can be totally directed at real, substantive work when you do not have to spend time looking over your shoulder. No need to spend time making certain that what was promised is delivered; what is expected in fact comes true. No one has to spend precious mental or emotional energy trying to figure out spoken innuendo or suspicious actions or trying to weasel around political minefields. "People within Ritz-Carlton Hotels not only operate with the absolute unwavering integrity," says John Dravinski, GM of the Ritz-Carlton Laguna Niguel. "They honor each other and insist others do as well. Bottom line: People here enjoy being kind to each other."

Honorable environments make clean dealings easy. Working in a setting where honor is a virtue better enables employees to look ahead always toward exciting, compelling goals, not back and forth and behind like prey nervously waiting for predator. In a trusting environment grounded in trusting relationships, roadrunners are able to scamper and soar with equal ease.

The Best People Flock to You

Honorable environments and honorable people attract the best talent—light attracts light. While there may be some truth in the idea of "no honor among thieves," today's environment teeming with no-secrets Web sites, special prosecutors, and class action lawsuits has surfaced a new allegiance to squeaky-clean and wholesome standards.

Talented people are not interested in having their hard-earned efforts thwarted by distractions like investigations, suspicion, or sleepless nights feeling guilty for what they tolerated or uneasy being associated with colleagues who sleep just fine. Roadrunners like being associated with scrupulous people. They know the bottom line must be realized without crossing the line. They avoid situations they know to be base or corrupt. One young recruit at State Farm Insurance put it this way: "I had great job offers from a lot of really successful companies. My mother does not have a clue what my job entails. But this is the only organization I considered which she would be proud of what the company stood for."

They also seek honest environments, where people tell the truth and leaders walk their talk. Roadrunners have little patience with political BS and backdoor, behind-the-back shenanigans.

Wile E. pours a can of birdseed into a nice pile on the road, next to a cactus. On the cactus he places a jar labeled "One-fifth Acme Bumble Bees," with a string attached to the cork. The Road Runner runs up to the seeds and begins pecking. Wile E. pulls the cork out of the bottle. The swarm of bees flies out of the bottle, hovers for a second over the Road Runner, then heads straight for Wile E., attacking and stinging him!

No Need for Snoopervision

Virtuous environments can be governed without inspection and managed without close supervision. In the words of a former Duke Energy CEO, the late Bill Lee, "We hire people who have a keen sense of what is right. We support a work environment in which people who do the right thing become the valued role models. We make 'doing the right thing' a standard of operation. Pretty soon, you have a company of people policing themselves and each other. It comes down to having people who drive the speed limit without a fuzz buster or a cop on the corner."

Roadrunner environments have very few rules. There *are* guidelines, which help efficiency, but few regulations and certainly no dictums. Roadrunner organizations are run by scrupulous people who simply honor a set of values. They not only do what's right; they have a clear and collective sense of what "right" means. They act according to conscience, not official decree.

And what makes an honorable organization? A power-full culture! A culture that is "full of power" is one with lots of people who feel strong and able. In fact, a power-full culture is an environment from which people draw strength in order to be involved, choose, act, cause change, create value. In coyote organizations, one person or a small cadre of persons is presumed to be powerful. Indeed, in such organizations new recruits who initially feel strong and excited eventually find their strength and spirit diluted, diminished by the organizational nonsense they have to wade through.

The irony of it all is that the coyote manager doesn't see that today's technological advances can make anyone powerful; all that's needed is an organization that supports the power that technology wants to bestow on the individual. Leonard Liu, CEO of Walker Interactive Systems, understands. Walker software products use Internet technology to allow their customers' employees (and any other constituencies, internal or external) to access any kind of up-to-the-minute financial information without going to a "boss," an accounting department, or anyone else. You want our net income status, you want a breakdown of working capital by receivables and inventory, you want a P&L breakdown per site, per truck, per route? Then click on a mouse. Listen to Liu's view of the world: "The beauty of the Internet is not the Internet itself. It is the development environment. It's an environment that enables any person on earth to develop his own creation and be able to make it available to everyone."

The Road Runner Is True to His Character

Ever notice how the Road Runner zooms so fast he looks like he's not even touching the desert floor? The Road Runner is light on his feet. And he is light because he carries no baggage. He has no guilt, no worry, and no anxiety . . . just unencumbered flow.

Wile E. loses because of drag. Ego and pride give him drag. Avarice and greed give him drag. Leaders and organizations are no different. Those who become full of themselves get weightier and falter. The business landscape is littered with the carcasses of dead organizations who thought they had armed themselves well against market realities.

The Greek word for "character" means "engraved." The Road Runner engraves his style on our hearts through his character. While Chuck Jones's selection of a roadrunner as the light side of the classic pursuit may have been serendipitous, it is inspired. Native Americans viewed the roadrunner with great respect as a symbol of good luck. Plains Indians hung the skin of a roadrunner over the door of their dwellings to ward off evil spirits. The Tarahumara Indians ate the roadrunner to achieve endurance and speed. Tribes of California Indians used feathers from a roadrunner in their headdresses as a tool of protection. But the ultimate tribute to this unique bird is in Mexican folklore, which insists it is not the stork that brings babies, but the roadrunner!

There is another connotation of "character" relevant here. A "character" in the traditional view of organizational life was an entity to be shunned. When someone labeled someone "a real character," the tag bordered on pejorative. It implied maverick, oddity, eccentric—or even a weirdo. The truth is great organizations and great units are spawned by great characters. Breakthroughs and record-bustings are generally done by characters . . . those wild ducks who march to their own drum.

Talk to anyone who's done something really interesting in the marketplace—Ted Turner of TBS, Michael Dell of Dell Computer, Jeff Bezos of Amazon.com—and you'll find someone who was labeled "crazy" or "insane" by pundits, analysts, academics, and today's competitors. Talk to anyone who's done something really interesting and provocative within an organization, and you'll find someone labeled as "weird" or "loony." They're characters in the purest sense of the word: individuals focused on creating and growing something new, in the most honest sense of the word.

In the coyote world of management, characters are shunned. Max Weber, who many years ago developed the entire model of bureaucracy (the coyote's bible), observed that "A flood of mistrust, sometimes of hatred, above all moral indignation, regularly opposed itself to the first innovator." Still does, in coyote organizations. In the roadrunner world of management, characters are embraced. That loony idea championed by that oddball may be what propels us to new competitive heights if we listen to it, develop it, test it.

Characters with character focus on improving, creating, shaping—not on destroying others or enhancing their self-image at someone else's expense. Character breeds focus and honesty. Political gamesmanship, deception, and weasel tactics are simply clutter. There's no need or time for it. There's cool stuff to be done. Accordingly, they threaten people with their strength, foresight, and commitment. They're also the ones who get things done and build new value. When he was an executive producer with *NBC Nightly News*, Steve Friedman advised his troops as follows: "I believe the people who work below you should love and admire you, and the people who work above you should think you're somewhat insane. They should have a bit of a pause, a bit of nervousness, before they pick up the phone to call you."

One of the world's leading distributors of aftermarket motorcycle and power sports vehicles is Fort Worth–based Tucker-Rocky Distributing. The company made a decision to go from twelve U.S. distribution centers to eight larger and more intelligent centers. Their move was not unique, particularly since the original twelve centers had evolved through evolutionary acquisition and therefore lacked consistent standards and up-to-date technology. What was unique was the manner in which President Frank Esposito elected to communicate their decision to the marketplace.

"There will likely be many rumors and rampant speculation," Esposito said in a telephone conference with the media. "However, please accept my promise that I have just given you all of the facts as they are known today. This is the total package of information—complete and honest." The coverage in the industry media was supportive and accurate. The media knew Frank. Frank is a roadrunner. So, if Frank said it was so, you could take it to the bank.

The Road Runner Is Grounded . . . Literally!

The Road Runner views Wile E. with curiosity, never with disdain or fear. No matter how deceitful the Coyote is, the Road Runner never retaliates in kind. How can this scrawny bird operate with such confidence against the much larger, mightier Coyote? It's a combination of Jones's magic with biological fact: The Road Runner is well grounded. Rather than taking a flighty route, he draws his power from the ground.

Wile E. is pulling back on a huge rubber band, attached to two stakes in the ground. Walking backward, pulling, pulling, pulling, stretching the rubber band to the limit. The Road Runner is standing right behind him. "Beep Beep," he says. Wile E. turns around and makes a grab for the bird. The Road Runner doesn't run away, doesn't even move, and the rubber band snaps back, flinging Wile E. the opposite way. He shoots through a tunnel and gets smashed by a train.

Chuck Jones developed several guidelines for cartoonizing these two characters to ensure consistency over time. One of Chuck's rules was, "The Road Runner must stay on the road; otherwise, he would not be called a '*road*runner.'" Likewise, organizations and leaders must figuratively stay grounded in their code of values. When Archimedes discovered the principle of leverage he said, "Give me a staff with length enough and a place whereupon to stand, and I will move the world." The Road Runner dramatically moves Wile E.'s world because he is anchored in his "place whereupon to stand."

Example: Back in 1985, while assisting Tom Peters in delivering a multiday executive retreat, Oren listened to a story that still reverberates years later. Marty Davidson, President of Southern Pipe & Supply (an independent wholesale distributor of plumbing supplies headquartered in Meridian, Mississippi), had built a loyal and growing customer base of builders and contractors through his company's commitment to service. One day Davidson received a call from a customer complaining that a $2.50 part had been left out of his shipment. The customer was in southern Louisiana and would have to keep a crew idle until the part arrived. It was too late for overnight delivery.

Without hesitation, Davidson put the part into the hands of an employee and got the employee on the next plane to New Orleans, where he delivered the part and then stayed overnight before returning home.

Was Davidson driven by some official service guarantee or legal obligation? Nope. What was the cost to Southern Pipe & Supply? Over $1,000. What possessed Davidson to take what any cost accountant would see as a foolish move? The answer is not the fanatical customer loyalty and word-of-mouth marketing that occurred as a result of Davidson's decision—those were the happy consequences. The answer—the reason he did it—in a phrase, his values.

"I have learned one thing that has made my business a success," says Davidson. "You cannot live your values only during the good times. The real test is to live them during the bad times. Besides, the $2.50 part incident was a good way to remind everyone in my shop about what is really important around here."

The Road Runner Follows His Own Code

The Coyote yields to his basic nature . . . the imprinting of coyote instincts from time immemorial. The Road Runner rises to a higher ideal. He operates according to a code, not an imprint. The Road Runner is pure because he pursues honor. He wastes no time or energy associating with baseness. It is not an arrogance; it is a choice—a discipline. Aristotle said, "Excellence is an art won by training and habituation. We are what we repeatedly do. Excellence, then, is not an act, but a habit." The Coyote yields to his weaker nature; the Road Runner wakes up his better side. He respects a conscience that operates according to an ever-refining code. Here are its key elements.

Focus on Your *Essence*, Not Your Enemy

The Road Runner focuses on being his absolute best. He is not preoccupied with competing with Wile E. It is not that he is oblivious to the Coyote's presence. In fact, he always seems to know exactly where Wile E. is hiding. But the Road Runner is more the alert bystander than anxious competitor. Wile E. is simply not the driving force in his life.

"When we gave up trying to 'beat Pepsi,'" said the late Coca-Cola CEO Roberto Goizueta, "and focused instead on our mission of 'bringing a Coke product within arm's length of every human being on the planet,' our market began to increase." Ed Wessing, CEO of American HomePatient in Nashville, puts it this way: "When competitor-watching becomes an obsession, you are in serious jeopardy of running off the road to success."

Remember the day you stopped being preoccupied with what your mother or father thought? It doesn't matter whether you were fourteen or forty-four. The point is that that day probably ushered in a new era of independence when you realized your parents were not preoccupied with what you thought of them either! "We've never tried to be like other airlines," says quintessential roadrunner Herb Kelleher, Chairman of Southwest Airlines. "From the very beginning we told our people, 'Question it. Challenge it. Remember that decades of conventional wisdom has sometimes led the airline industry into huge losses.'"

Do No Harm

The Road Runner is not obsessed with deliberately injuring or harming his adversary, though he is often amused by the many ways the Coyote does himself in.

Wile E. is set to fire an "Ahab Harpoon Gun." The Road Runner runs by and Wile E. fires. The harpoon shoots, but the rope attached to it wraps around the Coyote's leg, completely missing the target, Wile E. is dragged away by the harpoon over cacti and rocks. Finally, he rights himself and untangles from the harpoon rope. While concentrating on the rope, the harpoon goes off the cliff. Wile E. realizes he's about to fall so he grabs the rope again. The harpoon goes through a drainpipe and back on the road, dragging Wile E. with it. The harpoon continues over another cliff, finally hitting the side of a rock wall. Wile E., still holding on to the rope, swings down into a train tunnel. The train comes rushing out, smashing the Coyote back onto the ledge. Wile E., now with knees buckling, seeing stars, breathing heavily, wipes his brow and looks over the edge of the cliff. The Road Runner runs up behind him, looks at the audience, looks at the pitiful Wile E., looks back at the audience, and holds up a sign which reads, "I just don't have the heart. Bye!"

Roadrunner companies are vigilant in avoiding harmful actions, even to the point that Herman Miller Furniture commits to not using tropical woods from endangered rain forests or that Levi Strauss commits to using nondyed natural fiber in their jeans.

Roadrunners' concerns are not about "killing" or "crushing" their competitors—especially when the competitors are bigger, stronger, and better armed. It is a waste of energy, a drain on the kinds of creativity that will allow you to shape and lead a new market or project. The focus of roadrunners is to do something new and exciting and to achieve excellence in execution—catapulting over those seemingly invincible competitors. Ted Turner was not obsessed with "crushing" ABC, CBS, and NBC. Bill Porter at E*Trade wasn't obsessed with "destroying" Merrill Lynch. Jeff Bezos at Amazon.com wasn't obsessed with "killing" Barnes and Noble or Borders Books. Yet, these are the organizations that set extraordinary records in terms of brand equity and stock value. As of May, 1999, Amazon.com had a market value of $22 billion, which exceeded Caterpillar and Alcoa (all this on sales of $610 million). With a 46 percent equity stake in drugstore.com, Amazon has been expanding into health care and pharmacies. Its business model—a cyberspace mall—is steadily unfolding. The Road Runner's approach and strategy to life is simple: Know your competitors, observe the landscape, act honorably, and thrive.

Maintain 100 Percent Full-Time, Beak-to-Tail Integrity

"There is no such thing as a minor lapse of integrity," said Tom Peters. Roadrunners are bone-honest. Roadrunners not only walk their talk, but they strut their talk. Their moves are unabashedly consistent with their mouths. "Your actions should loudly speak your words," exhorts Southwest Airlines Chairman Herb Kelleher. Roadrunners state their principles and priorities and then live them.

And integrity pays off. The U.S. corporations that have paid dividends for 100 years or more are those that make ethics a high priority. If you had invested $30,000 in a composite of the Dow Jones thirty years ago, your portfolio would be worth $134,000 today. Had you invested the same amount in twenty-one companies with a written code of ethics stating that serving the public was central to their being, your portfolio would be worth over $1 million today.

When You're On, Be ON

The full-of-power component which emits from roadrunner organizations and roadrunner leaders comes from a focused energy. When it comes time to be on—to perform—they are all there, wide awake. There is a commitment to bringing all you are to what you do every time you do it. Coyotes coast; roadrunners soar. Roadrunners hold themselves to a higher standard of energy, knowing that if they give to the world the best that they have, the best will come back to them.

Marti Cornejo McMahon, CEO of San Francisco–based Pacific Marine Yachts, owns a fleet of luxury yachts used primarily for corporate events. Her clients include AT&T, Genentech, Oracle, prime ministers, and rock stars. Coming to the U.S. as a child from El Salvador, she dreamed of starting her own company around boating. Back in 1981, as a single mother of three, she started with a shoestring budget, hundred-hour workweeks, and one small boat which could accommodate forty-nine people. Reflecting on her twenty years of designing and renovating boats, she says, "My mother taught me how to create something beautiful from absolutely nothing. I'm proud of offering the very best. I still scrub toilets and work the galley. I love my business, I love my customers, I love my employees. I do it all from the heart."

"Our clients call us 'go-getters,'" says Jeff Prendergast, CEO of Dallas-based Retirement Advisors of America. "We choose people who enjoy working in the wide-open gear. They challenge each other every day to be on your game. The energy spills over to what our clients see, feel, and get from us." A part of a roadrunner's ethic is a fire-in-the-belly enthusiasm for excellence.

Keep Your Promises

Reliability is the foundation of trust; trust is the glue of honorable cultures. Keeping our promises is about protecting the sacredness of commitments. A promise is a covenant of assurance. It is about caring enough to remember. Keeping agreements, according to Gay Hendricks and Kate Ludeman in their book *The Corporate Mystic,* is "joining forces with the creative power of the universe, the same power that makes oak trees where no trees were before. Having stepped into unity with the creative force in the universe, you need to make good on the creation or cancel it out cleanly. Otherwise, you are bucking the greatest power there is."

Honor Your Partners

One feature which distinguishes the Road Runner from Wile E. is the manner in which each treats the other. Wile E. views his culinary goal as if he is naive and gullible. The Coyote's ploys assume the Road Runner can be easily hoodwinked. Consequently, his gross miscalculation seduces him into assuming a position of haughtiness. The Road Runner by contrast treats the Coyote with respect. While he is amused, he never smirks. While he witnesses his opponent do himself in, he never gloats.

Honoring a partner is also about providing that person the elbow room to be . . . to be unique, to be different, to be special. Partnerships marked by possessiveness are relationships that cease to grow. Partners in an overprotected relationship may initially feel secure and therefore valued. However, in time they will come to view possessiveness as a form of suspicion or mistrust. An initial feeling of security will ultimately be transformed into one of disdain and an experience of being devalued.

Always Do it with Flair

Roadrunners avoid the mundane. They pursue a surprising, dramatic, "those people are nuts" style. The Road Runner sports feathers in crazy colors . . . steel blue, bronzy green, olive, light yellow. Even his eyes are showy—golden yellow surrounded by blue skin in front and a brilliant orange-red patch in back! The Road Runner proclaims flair in the midst of an otherwise plain-vanilla desert. His actions match his colors, like the "transformational leaders" Tom Peters wrote about who are "bizarrely focused, tell the truth, and live life on the lunatic fringe."

Roadrunner leaders and organizations amaze their associates and are incomprehensible to their competitors. And roadrunners don't take themselves seriously. They think funny and are the first to laugh. When situations get too heavy, they symbolically stick out their tongues and shout "Beep Beep!" at the world, just like Stevens Aviation and Southwest Airlines in their famous ad slogan conflict. Stevens, a small aviation sales and maintenance company in Greenville, South Carolina, had been using the slogan "Plane Smart" for a year before Southwest Airlines unknowingly began running its "Just Plane Smart" ad campaign. Rather than duke it out in the courts, Stevens Chairman Kurt Herwald and Southwest Chairman Herb Kelleher elected to arm-wrestle for the rights to the slogan in front of employees and the media. They turned a potentially ugly court scene into a fun-filled evening in a smelly, run-down wrestling palace in Dallas, complete with cheerleaders and hundreds of fans. Stevens won the match and, in the end, let Southwest use the slogan anyway. The $5,000 wager went to charity, and everyone went home happy that they worked for two roadrunner organizations.

"Whatever you can do or dream you can, begin in boldness," wrote the philosopher Goethe. "Boldness has genius, power, and magic in it." Roadrunner leaders and organizations know this instinctively. They rarely miss an opportunity to add their unique flourish to any undertaking.

Make Your Own Luck

Wile E. Coyote climbs higher than he cares to fall! Why? Because he believes in luck. His actions speak his beliefs that good fortune comes to the fortunate, and he is among the chosen. When he fails, he is not so much angry as confused.

The Road Runner knows that life is like gravity—it has no favorites. Therefore, success comes through what you make of life, not what it makes of you. Roadrunners are in charge of their universe; they can be optimists because it is their attitude that determines their altitude. What is, is; what was, was; and what will be is what roadrunners make it.

Since roadrunners create their fortunes, they are never the victims of misfortune. But being in charge of your desert still carries responsibility. It means being attentive to your surroundings. It also means staying fit... physically and mentally. Ever notice how quickly Wile E. is winded after a long chase? You never see the Road Runner out of breath!

Like firefighters running drills in preparation for a fire, roadrunners have a disciplined regimen of preparedness. They stay awake and sharp. They get themselves primed and do their groundwork, as Roy Spence, president of Austin, Texas, based ad agency GSD&M, says of Southwest Airlines: "Herb and his team have always succeeded on merit because they are well prepared—they do more research than anyone." They get the worm . . . every time.

The Nobility of the Roadrunner Leader

We believe that "being honorable" is an action, one that combines "being the best" with acting according to a code of ethics. Being honorable results in behavior deemed noble. "To be noble" is an effect. Noble is a distinction reflective of an admired, elevated state. Johnson & Johnson's honorable handling of the Tylenol incident was deemed noble by the marketplace. "Noble" is a label given to people who act honorably, in a fashion that reflects the best of humanity. It is not just about goodness; it is about *bold* goodness. It is not just about morality; it is about brave morality.

People without firm ground sink. And people without an internal compass of what is true and pure get lost along the way. Roadrunners always know "true north." Their self-confidence comes from their self-awareness. "If I lose my honor," Shakespeare has Antony tell Octavia before the battle with Augustus, "I lose myself." Confucius wrote: "The superior man [aka the Road Runner] understands what is right; the inferior man [aka Wile E. Coyote] understands what will sell."

Noble roadrunner leaders are grounded and laced in complete, total, wall-to-wall, no-exceptions integrity. Roadrunner leaders stand on integrity; they are constructed of integrity, they reek of integrity. Integrity is the color they are painted, and true blue is a very bright blue, seen for miles around. Their integrity is as uncompromising as Abe Lincoln walking miles to return change from a transaction.

Roadrunner leaders show their nobility when they courageously turn their backs on shady deals or unscrupulous actions. They leave behind a strong and lasting legacy of integrity, honesty, and virtue on all those they influence. They never, ever, engage in any action that would leave even a tiny implication of impropriety or inference of shady intention. Roadrunner leaders perpetually lace their behavior with a passion for doing the right thing, even if another course of action might be more expedient, more popular, or more profitable.

What all this means is that in the Age of the Road Runner, it will be the honorable organizations that thrive, organizations respected for both their capabilities and their integrity, organizations that are honest, organizations focused on a noble cause. These organizations will attract and retain the best talent. These are the organizations that will differentiate themselves from the mob of their competitors. These are the organizations that will stand above the riffraff of coyotes in this global economy.

A coyote organization acts as if it has a finite amount of power, and individuals jockey to snare and hoard as much of it as possible; the ones at the "top" corner the market on it. Envy and distrust bubble up. Pernicious internal power battles are endemic. The notion of a collaborative noble cause becomes lost and the notion of honesty and candor becomes a liability. A roadrunner organization or unit, in contrast, has a culture where power is steadily expanding and available for the taking. Power is not seen as a zero-sum game. As people help one another get stronger, the organization becomes stronger.

Noble organizations and teams are by no means perfect. We all fall from grace from time to time. To err is not only human; it's roadrunner human, and organizations are, above all, human systems. But temporary mistakes never deter their roadrunner leaders from pursuing a proper path. Occasional, unintentional acts of indiscretion carry a lesson for improvement and a reminder that the noble always carry a heavy dose of humility and not a trace of arrogance.

BEEP! BEEP!

BIRDSEED

- Create a culture of total integrity, a place where leaders are bone-honest and where genuine interpersonal trust permeates.
- Call a halt to phony agreement. Encourage honest, candid dialogue. When associates publicly acquiesce to "yes" but privately feel "no" in their hearts, everyone loses.
- Never participate in gossip or backbiting. Honorable cultures work because they are filled with trust.
- Hire people with a reputation for having impeccable ethics. Get rid of brownnosing yes-men. If a leader has a yes-man, one of them is redundant! Publicly affirm acts that reflect honor and integrity.
- Get rid of hyper-legalistic, self-protective, arm's-length pseudo "partnerships." The opportunity for exceptional collaboration to achieve extraordinary goals is what attracts roadrunners.

Tail Feathers: A Roadrunner Standing on Principle

Sharon Allred Decker is the President of Doncaster, a division of Tanner Company and a retailer of high-end women's clothing. Headquartered in Rutherford, North Carolina, the company has over 2,000 reps around the country. The 1998 Chair of the Charlotte Chamber of Commerce, she has also served as Vice President of Customer Service for Duke Energy, where she turned a stodgy, conservative utility known for its mediocre service into the number one service provider in the country and 1999's most admired utility (according to a *Fortune* magazine study). She is a dynamic, groundbreaking leader, famous for creating cultures laced with passion and integrity.

What does being a roadrunner leader mean to Sharon? It starts with knowing what's important to you and to your unit or organization and never wavering from the values and principles you hold dear. It means, in her words, "always knowing true north."

> A roadrunner leader is willing to risk it all for their values. At Duke Power, we were creating a totally different service culture. We were trying to fundamentally change our relationship with our customers. My role was to encourage thousands of people to take a giant leap of faith into waters in which we had never swum.
>
> Roadrunner leaders live their integrity in very obvious ways. We live in a time when people are begging for folks to be honest . . . to be real and human. I don't believe you can really be a pacesetter, a change initiator, a visionary without a basic wellspring of character. The true leaders are those who can ground their vision with character.

Roadrunner leaders are also those who are strong enough to show their respect and regard for the people they work with. "Care for the people you are entrusted to lead," Sharon advises. "You are not their mother or father, but care for them passionately. They must feel our love as much as they feel your leadership." But don't lose sight of the horizon, the bigger picture, the vision, she cautions.

> Leaders remind people of the vision and encourage them to go for it. Coyotes will want you to spend your energy on the minutiae. Be a role model for thinking about work in radically new ways. Work can no longer be restricted to a physical place or time. We have to think about work in lunatic ways, creative and far out. That means being a great communicator . . . especially a great listener.

Know your principles and stick to them. Keep your vision sharp and clear, and manifest it every way you know how. Show your true colors in everything you do. Don't be afraid to be real and human, to show your care and concern—even love—for those you lead. There are stiff challenges, even for the most promising aspiring roadrunners.

What advice would Sharon offer when the going gets rough? Her reply was quintessential roadrunner:

> Pace yourself. Even roadrunners have to stop for water . . . and nourishment. If the passion is there, the energy is there. But with challenge after challenge, you can get a little weary. You have to take care of yourself if you expect to have energy enough to take care of others. Roadrunners enjoy the race so much they can forget to rest. So, exemplify good balance. Finally, work to be remembered for who you were, not just what you did. The legacy of great leaders is their character.

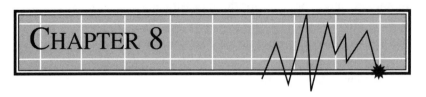

Curiosity
Mastery Is the Magic

The enthusiastic audience suddenly hushes as the lights dim and the curtains majestically open. A tuxedo-clad magician stands on a colorful stage behind an array of colorful props. Soon his sleight-of-hand exhibition has pigeons in air, rabbits in hat, and audience in awe. Is it his mysterious incantation, the snap of his fingers, or some unexplainable freakish feat that defies the laws of "that's not possible" rationality?

It is magic! And the genius of magic is not simply about sleight-of-hand trickery. True magic is the result of triple mastery . . . mastery of *method*, mastery of *medium*, and mastery of *market*. Tricks may draw a few passersby on the sidewalk or amuse kids at a birthday party, but only magic . . . real magic . . . can fill an auditorium. Every time Wile E. scratches his head in puzzlement, he gets a reaffirmation that he has just been snookered by more than a clever trick . . . it was some kind of magic.

Wile E. is up on a big mountain where the road ends at a sheer dropoff. He places a screen at the end of the road and paints a scene on the screen of the road continuing on, curving around the mountain. Wile E. tiptoes off to the side, turning around the road sign that reads, "Danger: End of Road." The Road Runner runs up, runs right into the scene, and runs around the mountain. Wile E. jumps onto the road and scratches his head in puzzlement. He turns to the audience and puts his hands out as if to say, "How could this happen?" As he turns back, a huge truck drives from around the curve painted on the screen and runs Wile E. over. Wile E. gets up, clenches his fists, and runs into the screen, only to pierce it and plummet to the canyon floor.

It's scratch-your-head, how'd-he-do-that magic! And because Wile E. is no magician, his clumsy attempts to parrot the Road Runner's skills result in catastrophe—just like a coyote team or organization's plodding attempts to mimic the actions of a roadrunner competitor almost invariably wind up in disappointment. What do roadrunner magicians do?

Great magicians, like the Road Runner, master their *method*. The root of the ruse must be rehearsed repeatedly. Practice not only makes perfect; it allows the practitioner to focus on more than the performance. The "wow!" we use to appraise the magician is the exact same assertion Wile E. uses when he sees the Road Runner performing some inexplicable tour de force. Only the Road Runner knows it is neither mystery nor freak accident. The Road Runner can perform with pleasure and repose because he's a practiced pro. Mastery starts with a commitment to drill and rehearsal.

Great magicians, like the Road Runner, also master their *medium*. "It's all in the presentation," said famed magician David Copperfield in an interview. The making of magic includes the management of the energy field between the magician and the audience. Lights, sounds, pace, timing, and even smell combine to ensure the aura of awe. Wile E.'s tricks might work if he paid more attention to the setting in which they are attempted. He doesn't. He assumes the "plan" will work because it's logical. Wrong! In contrast, the Road Runner reads every environmental cue to craft an escape that would make Houdini marvel! Mastery involves managing the entire network that connects product with patron.

Finally, great magicians, like the Road Runner, master their *market*. They not only respect their audience; they spend focused effort keeping a grasp on what spectators expect and what makes them swoon. And they never stop learning, since they know that today's "oh, wow" will be tomorrow's "ho hum." Wile E. is perpetually surprised every time he experiences the Road Runner's seeming capacity to read the coyote's mind and anticipate his every move. Mastery includes knowing at any moment how the ultimate end user assesses enchantment.

Teams and organizations that keep customers astounded and coming back for more make magic the same way as the magician and the Road Runner. Magical results happen if the organization or team perpetually strives to master the skills needed to create a great service or product, to master the playing field, and to maintain a keen understanding of the marketplace.

Secrets of the Road Runner's *Method*: Wonder and Worth

The Coyote enjoys presenting his business card . . . it reads "Wile E. Coyote: GENIUS!" His choice says a lot about his arrogance as well as his dependence on the trappings of status. The irony is that his ends are completely at odds with his handle. Watch a few scenes of Wile E.'s brand of genius and you'll find yourself saying, "He made that same kind of mistake three scenes ago." He's clearly no genius! "Stupid is as stupid does," said Forrest Gump. And Wile E. seems to have a knack for "doing stupid."

The Road Runner approaches his world with a completely different orientation. He combines his spirit of wonder and wide-eyed curiosity with an enthusiastic vitality solidly focused on a ceaseless pursuit of worth. His curiosity is as conspicuous as Wile E.'s conceit. His forward-focused perspective (rather than a look-over-your-shoulder defensiveness) keeps him forever fixed on what's to come, not frustrated by what was. He is constantly adapting, adjusting, learning, remembering. The result is magic, as Wile E. can attest.

Every time Wile E. Coyote puts out a trick like free food or free photographs, the Road Runner comes over to inspect. Why? He's fully in tune with his environment and totally confident in his capacity to respond. He comes to peruse the latest ruse because he's a curious bird. Learning new things, exploring new venues, investigating oddball happenings in his environment—that's the nature of the bird. Mastery requires curiosity . . . a never-ending spirited receptivity, an openness to adventure and zealous inquiry. As Socrates wrote over 2,000 years ago: "Education is the kindling of a flame, not the filling of a vessel."

Roadrunner units and organizations are hardwired for perpetual learning. In the words of philosopher Eric Hoffer,

"In times of massive change, it is the learner [aka the Road Runner] who will inherit the earth, while the learned [aka Wile E. Coyote: Genius] stays inflexibly attached to a world which no longer exists." Roadrunner organizations, for example, capture knowledge on central, accessible interactive databases. VeriFone (credit card authorization), Buckman Labs (specialty chemicals), and Cemex (cement) invest heavily in networked information technology to allow anyone with questions to access knowledge and each other. Consulting firms like Bain and Company and Ernst & Young make "contribution to and utilization of the knowledge asset of the firm" a major part of performance review and compensation.

At Cemex, if a salesperson in one country has a problem and needs advice, he or she can throw up the question into the in-house cyberspace and receive responses from Cemex people around the world. At Ford, if a work team wants to minimize learning curve errors on a particular process, they can access the expert system database that documents what other teams in similar situations have done and learned. "If we only knew what we knew," observed one executive, "we could be three times more profitable than we are now."

The goal is constant learning. Corporations are even becoming universities. Several years ago First Union National Bank established First Union University. One of the tenets of First University is to give the learners choices and the ability to access learning when, how, and where they want it. Broadcast capability exists to over 2,000 branches and can cover topics from bond math to large conversion training events. Simple delivery tools enable a salesperson to access product tapes en route to a call, for instance, or a manager to get coaching tips online. "It is inexpensive, easy to update and duplicate, and very portable," according to Dr. Kathryn Heath, Director of First University.

Roadrunner organizations have leaders who ensure that attributes like ongoing growth, incessant improvement, and endless experimentation are their trademarks. Roadrunner units and organizations regard "incomplete" as an asset and "to be continued" as an attribute. Roadrunners consider every quest a pilot, every undertaking an experiment. They know that revering consistency is the last resort of the unimaginative.

Wile E. holds a can of "Acme Iron Pellets." He pours the pellets from the can into a mound and then pours a box of "Ajax Bird Seed" on top. Satisfied with his trap, he climbs upon a ledge hauling a fishing pole with a magnet attached to the end. The Road Runner runs up to the mound, smacks his beak, and starts pecking at the seed. Wile E. lowers the magnet. However, halfway down, the magnet is attracted to electrical wires and makes contact with them. The electric charge makes its way to Wile E. The power turns his nose into a light bulb, which he unscrews from his face and watches his nose light up.

Mastery is also about vitality and discipline. Roadrunners never stop practicing. Their incessant pursuit of their best keeps them forever honing skills, improving methods, and altering approaches. Learning is the high-octane fuel on which great masters race. While the outside world may proclaim mastery, roadrunner units are forever master*ing*! The spirit of "Road Runner" is a gerund, not a noun.

Wile E. paints a roadway, gets a sign which reads "Slow—School Crossing," and places it in the middle of the road. He disappears and then reappears wearing a blond wig with red bows and a green schoolgirl's outfit and skips across the road. The Road Runner goes by at full speed and blows Wile E. around the sign. Returning wearing a blond wig with red bows, the Road Runner stops and holds up a sign that says "Roadrunners Can't Read." Sticking his tongue out, he Beeps and races away.

Mastery takes the humility to be able to say "I don't know" and the curiosity to utter "Tell me more." Mastery takes the boldness to try the new and different. The Road Runner sticks his neck out. He shows chutzpah and spunk. In the face of a menacing coyote he grins! "If people never did gutsy and silly things," says Colleen Barrett, Executive Vice President of Southwest Airlines, "nothing really intelligent or creative would ever get done." When Vice President Al Gore visited Southwest, the advance team wanted to give Southwest questions for employees to ask Mr. Gore and suggested Southwest handpick the people to ask them. Colleen Barrett countered, "No, our people would be offended. We're not worried about who the Vice President calls on. Our people will be spontaneous; they will ask good, substantive questions, and they *will* be articulate!"

Roadrunner organizations, like Southwest Airlines, seek to strip censure and fault-finding from their culture. Censure can turn an open atmosphere into one of protection, caution, and guarded behavior. Without vulnerability there is no risk; without risk there is no experimentation and growth. Roadrunner organizations nurture cultures where people are proudly known by the quantity, quality, and magnitude of their interesting mistakes—like the division of a major organization we know that gives out an annual green weenie award, a coveted distinction bestowed on the person who, while attempting excellence, created a major failure which resulted in significant organizational learning. It is a valued badge of courage!

Mastery of *method* is also acquired through an enthusiastic pursuit of worth . . . as in premium, distinction, excellence. "Master" is a concept that belongs in the same lexicon as expert, virtuoso, maestro, or champion. It means going for the very best. GE Chairman Jack Welch says, "If you aren't striving to do your very best, you soon won't be doing at all." Roadrunners are never complacent, never rest on their laurels or rely on their track record. Roadrunners never slow down, never take the lazy route, never let their enthusiasm wane. "Beep Beep" is their animated, signature cheer . . . as if to proclaim to the desert, "Never shout one Beep when two will do!" Roadrunners give more.

The gift of learning has been a valuable competitive tool for Target, the retail chain that accounts for 75 percent of parent company Dayton Hudson's nearly $30 billion in revenues. Buyers from Dayton Hudson's upscale stores (like Marshall Field, Dayton's) attend the high-end fashion shows (off limits to bargain basement Target) and then share with their Target colleagues what they learn of style trends and directions. Target immediately develops its own private-label knockoffs, which are cheaper than the "real" clothes that the Dayton Hudson upscale stores feature. They do it so well even upscale shoppers frequent "Tar-jay."

Secrets of the Road Runner's *Medium*: Viewpoints and Trial Runs

Much of the humor in the Road Runner cartoons turns on the fact that the props Wile E. acquires from Acme always fail to help him snare his prey. And they always fail because of the coyote's tragic flaws. Wile E. never, ever misreads the instructions on the Acme box. In fact, he has method-mastery down pat. And he could never win a product liability lawsuit... Acme products never break down or fail to perform as they were intended.

Poor product quality is never the root of Wile E.'s latest embarrassing error. He invariably blows it when it comes to implementation because of his arrogant attitude and myopic perspective. His pomposity and pride blind him to the need for adapting the Acme gizmo to his particular situation. He fails to understand his context... the medium in which application must take place. Like a plow horse wearing blinders to force its focus on the row ahead, Wile E. misses the subtleties of his milieu. Seduced by his obsessive greed, he executes with his belly instead of his brain.

Now contrast the Road Runner's triumphant modus operandi. He always operates from the high road... constantly cognizant of the comprehensive outlook. He not only keeps his razor-sharp awareness trained on minute detail; he is sharp-sighted to the broad point of view. He delights in maintaining an open orientation to his surroundings, an optimism that keeps him equipped to capture good fortune. His perspective is one that is physically and spiritually elevated and open.

"Freeware" is an illustration of emerging roadrunner openness to learning. In early 1998, for example, Netscape posted the source code of the Nagivator browser (via Mozilla.org) and opened it up for developers anywhere to contribute to the next generation. Linux uses the same roadrunner high road. The Linux operating system, a Unix-based system "overseen" by original writer Linus Torvalds, is totally open and shaped daily by master contributors around the world.

Roadrunner organizations also fully understand the importance of a sharp yet broad perspective. High-potential managers at Marriott, for example, attend a respected week-long executive development program. The program faculty not only includes Marriott top execs and industry experts but philosophers and anthropologists. Sessions are interactive, provocative, and deeply engaging. Participants and instructors learn together as they explore present and future challenges from avant garde perspectives. "Our success in the next millennium," says Marriott Executive Development Director Jill Kallmeyer, "will require leaders who have breadth as well as depth, renaissance thinkers who can solve complex problems from an eclectic and sometimes unconventional point of view. We will be successful in the future if our leaders think beyond a hospitality perspective."

Computer Curriculum Corporation managers at a recent retreat put on a play to reenact a particularly challenging organizational issue. Participants dressed in costumes and videotaped the play to be aired later at a major management meeting. The comical video proved to be the impetus to new insight and creative problem-solving. "We solve thorny challenges," says VP Michael Somers, "by taking a sometimes wacky view of them." Finding the winning ingredients for success can come through how you look at the recipe.

The Road Runner is munching birdseed on the side of the road. On an overlooking cliff, Wile E. is holding a grenade directly over the bird. He drops it, but the grenade hits an electrical wire. The wire acts like a rubber band, stretching almost all the way down, but then shooting the grenade straight back at Wile E. Wile E. initially snickers when he drops the grenade, but when it comes back to him he frantically tries to put the pin back into the grenade. BOOM!

Mastery of medium also involves creating cultures bursting with tries, explorations, "what ifs," and "why nots?" Magicians try out signals, scenarios, and signs before settling on a setup. Creating that special ambience and developing that impeccable timing come through experimentation. Roadrunner units know full well that trials lead to mistakes and errors, but in the end they always prevail. "There's no pride of authorship on ideas in this company," says Houston-based Metamor Worldwide President Ken Johnsen, "since the ink can never dry on the success story we are writing." The secret is to fail fast, stumble forward, learn and fix, and share your learning with others.

Disney chairman Michael Eisner articulates the issue this way: "Mediocrity is the bane of existence. I'd rather have the most celebrated failure, along with the most celebrated successes, than a constant life of mediocrity. I've failed. I've made movies that were terrible. But one of the biggest failures a manager can experience is avoiding risk. When you're trying to create new things, you have to be on the edge of risk and failure. People want something new, and different, and unusual. The only way to deliver that is by breaking norms and taking risks."

Rich Teerlink, CEO of Harley-Davidson, begins many executive meetings with the declaration: "Here is something I screwed up on this week—and, what I learned from it." Each executive in his leadership team follows suit. The goal is not to foster true confessions from the guilty, but rather to create a platform for public recognition of humility and an openness for learning and team support.

"Fine for some folks," you may be saying, "but in our unit, you can't afford to have that 'fail fast' mind-set." Nobody is suggesting that you bet the bank on everything you do. But if your unit is not regularly making interesting mistakes, then you are not pushing the envelope. We all have comfort zones about three sizes too small. Roadrunners know that progress comes beyond the comfort zone. They pursue dissonance and discomfort, not security and stability and reaping the rewards. They are the ones doing the fast failing and fast learning.

Secrets of the Road Runner's *Market*: Customized and Special

How could a big old, hungry coyote keep missing a scrawny, unappetizing roadrunner? Bottom line: He fails to fully appreciate his pint-size adversary. His arrogance and superiority complex lead him to misjudge the Road Runner's talents. He assumes this bird is just like all the other desert morsels he continually chases and captures. When his pursuits fail to pan out, he follows the same attack plan . . . only harder. We see Wile E. scratch his head so often he should be bald. And his puzzling defeat is puzzling to the point that it drives him crazy! It's like Chuck Jones paraphrasing philosopher George Santayana: "A fanatic is one who redoubles his effort when he has forgotten his aim."

Organizations sometimes treat their market as Wile E. does. When Intel first released the Pentium chip, word got out that it had a tiny glitch. Customers asked for a replacement or refund. Intel concluded that only a very few customers with mega-computer systems could be hurt by the glitch and winnowed out the customers whose requests they would honor. Their other customers felt betrayed. Even after a furious public outcry, Intel stood by their plan with the same obstinacy Wile E. uses to follow an Acme blueprint.

In an *Inc.* magazine article entitled "My Biggest Mistake," then CEO Andy Grove finally acknowledged Intel's faulty decision: "We basically defied our consumer population. In retrospect, that was incredibly condescending and arrogant. . . . Now, I've learned that fighting with the consumers isn't a good idea." More recently, Intel was forced again to backtrack, this time in the face of the protest which accompanied the release of its Pentium III chip. Each chip had a "processor serial number," a ninety-six-digit security feature which would identify any user who logged onto the Internet. The crescendo of outcries over privacy invasions (the Electronic Privacy Information Center posted a logo on its Web site mocking the well-known "Intel Inside" insignia, saying instead, "Big Brother Inside") overwhelmed the company's explanations, and once again, Intel retreated.

But this time, they did it quickly, efficiently, and humbly. They did it in problem-solving collaboration with their critics—who, after all, represent many of the best and brightest in the high-tech environment. Bottom line: They honored their market. They learned. Unlike Andy Grove and his team, Wile E. never learns.

Magicians respect their audience, always seeking to understand their ever-changing needs and striving to surprise them by giving more than is expected or anticipated. Roadrunners, likewise, honor their market. As the coyote is packed with disdain, the Road Runner is filled with delight; while Wile E. focuses on crushing, the bird pursues soaring. The Road Runner is at one with the desert, using every fragment of his shifting surroundings to emerge triumphant.

Roadrunner organizations like Victoria's Secret hold customer focus groups in the cafeteria at the corporate headquarters in Columbus, Ohio, during lunch hour, making the priority and importance of market input clear to all. Duke Energy gets customers involved in company committees and study groups. Quad/Graphics, a high-quality printer of major magazines like *Ms., Time, Modern Photography*, and *Playboy*, invites customers directly onto the printing floor to learn . . . and to teach. Plastics molder Nypro and its customers (like Saturn and J&J) consciously learn from each other (technology, science, operations, and customer service).

Bristol Hotels and Resorts, a large hotel chain headquartered in Dallas, has done focus groups with the taxicab drivers who transport guests from the hotel to the airport. "We take curiosity to the highest plane possible starting at the top. Our President, John Beckert, is on the phone with guests almost every day," says Senior Vice President John Long-street. "We want to send a clear message to everyone—guests, associates, vendors—that we are always learning—always trying to get better. You can't improve what you don't know about. We believe that, no matter how successful we've become, the second we get arrogant is the beginning of the end. We do not want to be a success in our market, we want to master it—and, that means nonstop learning."

Curious roadrunners think; closed coyotes just react. Mastery is about using your brain rather than your trigger finger. This is not a plea for paralysis from analysis. It is counsel to reflect before you react. The Coyote might be lauded for his determination, but he loses during execution because he fails to think. He gets so enamored with his devious plot that he never thinks through how it will play out. Consequently, he comes off as aggressively dumb. Taking time for contemplation and deliberation could improve the probability of successful implementation.

Think about it. The Road Runner operates in an open desert . . . completely exposed, without weapons or protective gear. The Coyote, on the other hand, hides behind rock and bush, ready to aim his latest Acme gizmo at this scrawny bird. The Road Runner's edge is his magical mastery.

The Master Roadrunner Leader

Many years ago, as leadership expert and USC professor Warren Bennis tells it, legendary IBM CEO Tom Watson, Jr., put a young executive in a new venture. The executive worked very hard, doing the best he knew how, but managed to lose $10 million in a fairly short time. Watson asked to see the young exec. The story goes on with the executive entering the CEO's auditorium-size office and quickly saying, "I presume, sir, I am here to tender my resignation." To which Watson is reported to have replied, "Resignation, hell—I can't afford to fire you. I just spent $10 million training you." The story epitomized IBM's culture . . . excellence is to be celebrated, even if it sometimes starts with failure.

Roadrunner leaders foster a work culture that honors experimentation over procedure, ingenuity over compliance, and learning from failure over protecting the tried and true. "When we see that to learn," wrote Peter Senge in *The Fifth Discipline*, "we must be willing to look foolish, to let another teach us, learning doesn't always look so good anymore. Only with the support, insight, and fellowship of a community can we face the dangers of learning meaningful things."

Roadrunner leaders work hard to always communicate reality. They know that actions of authenticity are needed to level the learning field. If they show vulnerability, they create judgment-free relationships. Authority and rank are the enemies of learning and growth. Roadrunner leaders know if they demonstrate support and care, they bolster a crucial foundation for the risk-taking, make-a-bit-of-a-fool-out-of-yourself behavior necessary for meaningful growth. They encourage zany, out-of-the-box thinking and action.

Roadrunners know that being "normal," as in follow-the-rules conservatism, is a prescription for being the coyote's next meal. So, they pursue the "not normal." To paraphrase an old Waylon Jennings country music song, "I've always been crazy and it's kept me from going out of business." There is very little normal about a roadrunner. Real roadrunners don't look normal . . . they are multicolored in wild shades. Roadrunners don't sound normal . . . other birds sing and chirp! Roadrunners don't move normal . . . other birds fly. Roadrunners don't eat normal . . . their diet is lizards and snakes, not worms and bugs. When it comes to workaday thinking and practices, are you a roadrunner . . . or are you a coyote?

Roadrunner leaders know the spirit of a supportive community is one of authenticity and genuine care. They are willing to reveal their own challenges and frustrations confidently. They invite exploration and innovation by offering support, not rebuke or obstacles. They challenge without being challenging; they push for greatness without being pushy or parental. They foster a work environment that encourages associates to reassure, not reproach; to bolster, not to blame.

Roadrunner leaders assertively proclaim their excitement for learning. It's more than a role-modeling "got to"; it's more a dying-to-know "want-to" that launches their quest for wisdom. Roadrunner leaders are ardent students of life. They ask more questions, read more books, seek out more diverse thinkers, pursue more life-changing experiences than their counterparts. They put learning at the top of their agenda . . . and leave it there. They provide quick and noticeable affirmation to other enthusiastic learners in the organization. They teach, they mentor, and they learn. "Because the next generation of managers will face different, more complex realities," said Wal-Mart CEO David Glass in his 1999 address to 1,500 Sam's Club managers, "each of us needs to develop someone better than we are."

Roadrunner leaders who are curious are externally focused, aware, and in tune with their environment—which means they focus on the right things, the things that matter to their customers. Moreover, they are able to sniff out trends in new technology, new competitors, new threats, new products, new partnership opportunities, new extensions of current product lines—that's what roadrunners do so well that they're never taken by surprise.

The more an organization works to improve its methods, master its medium, and understand, anticipate, and respond to its markets, the more it has positioned itself to create hits. And the more the organization is on target, the greater its customers' loyalty. Enchanted customers, like an awed audience, refer business to you enthusiastically and forgive your slipups more readily. In such a dynamic partnership there are more opportunities for the organization to understand, anticipate, and respond to customer needs. This never-ending cycle enables an organization or unit to repeatedly deliver its magic time and time again and, in time, become a role model for others to chase.

Mastery is magical. And since an organization's ability to learn faster than its competition is its *only* sustainable competitive advantage, mastery is also *the* magic. Mastery is far more than the acquisition of wisdom. Mastery comes with an attitude . . . a roadrunner attitude. Mastery seekers take an egalitarian, accepting stance in all they do. Mastery seekers are quick to accept and slow to critique. Mastery seekers never stop being awed, surprised, or excited. Like the Road Runner, they outrun by outlearning.

BIRDSEED

- Institute a practice of frequent sabbaticals. Help people identify what they want to learn and link them with the resources that can help them do it.
- Have people who attend outside conferences and workshops share their learning with others.
- Give your most demanding customers opportunities to speak their mind with anyone and everyone in your unit. Invite out-of-the-ordinary people from diverse disciplines to address your work teams.
- Hire a clipping service to track topics of interest to employees. Promote the circulation of books and magazines. Put racks with a wide assortment of journals and magazines in the bathrooms.
- Start an audiotape library for people to check out and listen to going to and from work. Create an electronic knowledge network (intranet).
- Join and contribute to project teams that are interdisciplinary. Don't just stick in your safe domain, your own work group or function. Volunteer for something you've never done before.

Tail Feathers: A Roadrunner Who Transcends Time

∙∙

The first thing some people notice about Bernard Rapoport is his age: eighty-two. Then they promptly forget about it as they try to keep up with this hyper-vigorous man who runs rings (physically and intellectually) around people decades his junior. Bernard Rapoport, or B as he's affectionately known to employees and high-profile politicians alike, is the founder, Chairman, and CEO of American Income Life Insurance, based in Waco, Texas.

In order to understand B and the company he's poured his heart and soul into, you have to understand his personal history. As he says, in his Texas twang, "You never know me for more than five or ten minutes and you know I'm the child of a Russian Jewish revolutionist." B's father, David Rapoport, was a passionate socialist who escaped czarist Russia in 1912 and settled in San Antonio. He never lost his political zeal, his dedication to labor union solidarity, and his commitment to making the world a better place. And he passed his philosophy along to B.

Understand this and you understand what happens from 1951 to the present.

After graduation from the University of Texas, B sold insurance. In 1951 he founded American Income Life Insurance to serve a unique niche: unions. The company has grown to nearly a billion dollars in assets and provides insurance products to more than two million individuals in North America, representing over 20,000 unions. In 1994 it was sold for over $500 million to holding company Torchmark, which gives Rapoport free rein to run it. The peddler's son has hit the rags-to-riches American dream.

How has he done it? Hang out with Rapoport and the company for a while and soon you see the values emerge, values that he has been instrumental in driving hard for forty years.

Integrity and honesty: Straight and candid communication inside the company—no political secrecy, no gamesmanship, no back stabbing, and with customers, no deceptions, no lies, no tricks, no games.

Commitment to a cause: American Income waives (not defers, waives) premium payments during authorized strikes, as they did during the big UAW strike against GM in 1998, for example. The company also waives premiums for ninety days in the event of a layoff, sponsors food banks for striking members, provides scholarships for children of union members, conducts voter registration drives, and publishes the national *Labor Letter.*

Strong standards, goals, and financial incentives: B is blunt with his agents about responsibility, standards, opportunities, performance, and leadership: "I am fighting for my job and I want you to fight for yours! I don't want anyone's mundane excuses as you say *quota* is a harsh word. You bet it is harsh, but so is leadership. It is tough. We are looking for solutions, not excuses." The payoff, as he repeats over and over, is to be part of a great cause and make yourself rich. "More than 90 percent of agents who have retired over the last forty-seven years have done so without having to change their standard of living," he says. Of the twenty-five top people in the company, he is immensely proud that eighteen are millionaires— and he's talking real cash flow, not stock options. Many others throughout the company earn six figures annually.

Accessibility and caring: B is directly available to *anyone* in his company through face-to-face, phone, fax, or e-mail (including weekends). But more than that, he shows that he cares about his employees and his clients. As corny as it sounds, "love" is not too strong a word; ask his people. Even as he drives them à la football coaching legend Vince Lombardi, they know that, like Lombardi, the man cares for them personally in a way that few leaders do. He constantly challenges his own leadership team to model this behavior with questions like "Have you made that new agent really feel special?" "Have you demonstrated that we are a caring company?"

So, here is a roadrunner who transcends age, a man who still plays tennis every morning, who reads to elementary school children once a week, and who was rated by *Fortune* magazine as one of the twenty-five top philanthropists in the country. He is a man who is an active Democratic party contributor, a personal friend of the Gores and the Clintons, and yet is respected by politicians and businesspeople of every political persuasion. At this point in his life, his management philosophy is about the need for change. Over and over, like a broken record, he tells his people, "We've got to break with the past," "If it ain't broke, start fixing it anyway," ending with a ringing "I want my life changed!"

I have finally come to realize that there is never a final resting place for those who have that urge, that necessity, that unrestrained impulse to do better and to be better. Those who strive to break out of the shell that constrains most people find that they never experience that sense of boredom so many complain of. It just doesn't happen to those who want to build an organization because it is change that keeps us alert and excited. We only need to accept change as a positive endeavor in the continued growth of any organization to eliminate any constraints we may have felt.

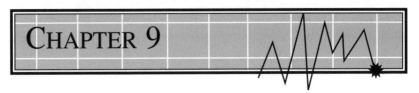

CHAPTER 9

Maverick
Breakthrough Is the Road to Prosperity

We know the Road Runner is agile, imaginative, smart, and fleeting. If all that weren't daunting enough for his predator, he has yet another, even more extraordinary, attribute that practically guarantees he'll never get caught.

Wile E. paints a center divider on the road and then paints a turn in the road, all the way to the face of a mountain. He then paints an image of a tunnel on the mountainside. Wile E. hides himself and the paint bucket behind a rock. We hear the sound of the Road Runner approaching, getting louder, and then we see the Road Runner go right through the "tunnel." Wile E. emerges from his hiding place, puzzled and angry. He clenches his fist, steps back to get a running start, races toward the "tunnel," and smashes right into the mountain. As he's wobbling around from the blow, the Road Runner comes back through the "tunnel" and runs right over him.

What's this particular characteristic the Road Runner has that Wile E. doesn't? We call it "BREAKTHROUGH." Roadrunners—birds or businesspeople—are able to break through barriers that are seemingly insurmountable, leaving their rivals baffled and angry, as in "How'd they do that?" Over the past two decades, people like Michael Dell, Ted Turner, Bernie Ebbers, Fred Smith, Sam Walton, Herb Kelleher, Debbi Fields, and Bill Porter have broken through the barriers of conventional wisdom and preexisting market conditions to reinvent the world of computer delivery (Dell Computer), news delivery (CNN), telecommunications services (WorldCom), overnight package delivery (FedEx), general merchandise retail (Wal-Mart), air transportation (Southwest), cookies (Mrs. Fields Cookies), and stock trading (E*Trade). The returns on these breakthroughs—in terms of profit, stock, and brand equity appreciation—were, and often remain, exceptional.

In the new millennium, expect more and more vendors in every market, and expect them to be offering me-too products, services, and distribution systems, all of which act to lower their individual margins, earnings, and shares. The winners will be those who break away from the pack and play by a completely different set of rules. These few champions will be those who understand—as the Road Runner does—that *breakthrough* is the road to prosperity.

Breakthroughs Begin with *Breaking* Something

Consider Michael Dell. His experience as a university freshman was a bit different from ours. When we were freshmen, our anxieties revolved around grades, our obsessions around members of the opposite sex. Dell's attention was elsewhere (which may explain why he's worth billions and we're not). He saw that computer hardware was becoming a commodity and that even an eighteen-year-old could make money by upgrading old machines. That same year he graduated to the next level—buying components, assembling the entire PC, stamping a "Dell" brand on the product, and selling it directly to consumers at a 15 percent discount.

That was the breakthrough, the new business model. Dell shattered many conventional computer marketplace concepts. First, he built PCs to customer specifications, breaking with the tradition the competitive computer maker world used of convincing customers to buy what they built. Second, he went virtual. He pulled pieces together from other people's inventories as he needed them, instead of managing a large finished-product inventory created by a large manufacturing staff.

Finally, Dell sold directly to consumers through the mail. He broke with the standard practice of relying on retailers, distributors, and resellers, all entities needing to be managed and funded by the sticker price of the product. Those breakthroughs launched the company in 1984, and since then, in true roadrunner fashion, Dell the computer and Dell the man have remained impatient with business as usual.

Is there a payoff to this sort of breakthrough approach? You be the judge. In early 1999, they had revenues of over $18 billion and were the number one seller of PCs in the U.S. and corporate markets, the number one seller of Intel-based machines in the education market, and the number 2 provider (after Compaq) for the home market. Net income rose 55 percent to $1.4 billion. And, oh yes, the stock has appreciated modestly since 1990, a mere *29,000 percent.*

Many outsiders fail to understand Dell's success. They attribute Dell's steep sales and share rise to low pricing. Low pricing is a nonbreakthrough way of competing, and it usually wreaks havoc with margins and customer loyalty, for the customer who comes to you for the low price will leave you for a lower one, and that's *after* beating your price down. Actually, Dell appeals largely to the high-end corporate and home user, the ones who want a fully loaded machine to tackle a variety of sophisticated technology needs. But within that high-end spectrum, Dell offers a terrific price. Hence, it's not price that drives Dell; it's value as defined by the customer. That's where Dell's breakthroughs come in.

The company understands that competitive advantage in the emerging economy is no longer dependent on "mass," as in mass production, mass marketing, and mass distribution. Nor is it dependent on uniformity, standardization, and scale. To be sure, Dell has built great efficiencies into its systems, and it capitalizes on scale in parts purchasing—but the company understands that the keys to business success lie in addressing each customer's individual needs and idiosyncrasies. It's a way to differentiate yourself from competitors, to forge direct, unfiltered long-term relationships and thus engender customer loyalty, and to add genuine value to commodity products and services.

So, here's what happens when a purchasing manager of a Fortune 500 company clicks on Dell's Web site—or, more likely, her own company's secured customized Web site built by Dell and presented in the company's own language. The manager can pick the chip, box, power, peripherals, and any other features and get real-time price information with each step. Once she makes her selection, she gets a confirmation and delivery date within five minutes—and there is a strong likelihood that her machines will be ready for overnight delivery within thirty-six hours.

The Dell magic has captured individual buyers as well. Chip owns four Dells, and he doesn't buy them because they work better than other computers. They work fine, but he buys them because they customize the product and personalize his experience in dealing with them. He feels that his specs literally drive their production process, and he's right. They make *his* computer, not anyone else's. And he can send them his specs via fax or Web, but he prefers to place an order on the phone because Dell has his entire history on file and the sales rep can pull up that history and give him personal advice—"They make me feel like I am their *only* customer," he says.

Breakthrough! Over much bigger hardware competitors. Breakthrough! Over entrenched channels of reseller distribution and retail sales that dominate the PC industry. Breakthrough! Through an "inviolable" business model whose premise is "build a standardized product and sell it through mass markets." Breakthrough! Through the conventional wisdom that nobody can make real money on the Net just yet.

If you are not willing to break something, go back to bed! Roadrunners don't stand on tradition; they rebelliously buck the trend, change the pattern, crack the code, and throw away the mold. Roadrunners enjoy "in your face," Texas-style dealings. They search for the principle to be reversed and the model to be challenged. When they hear "can't" it is their wake-up call to prove otherwise.

Consider the following fact about real roadrunners: Roadrunners eat rattlesnakes. Extensive research on the habits of roadrunners reveals two methods for this courageous and frightening task. The direct attack is accomplished by rushing the rattler, feinting and kicking up dust until the snake strikes. The roadrunner dodges, turns, and delivers continuous lightning-speed pecks on the rattler's head until it dies. The cactus-armor-shield technique entails the roadrunner holding a cactus pad as a shield, causing the striking snake to be pierced by the thorns. After repeated but futile strikes, the exhausted snake, covered with thorns, gives up and is killed by the roadrunner. There has never been a documented case of a roadrunner losing to a rattlesnake.

The End of Incrementalism

Increasingly, in the emerging Age of the Road Runner, it will be the quantum Dell-like leaps, not the small sustained gains, that will define genuine business prosperity. Certainly, continuous improvement of today's processes and products is a necessity and will always remain so. But increasingly, plain-vanilla incrementalism in thinking and action will at best allow a company to barely survive. Roadrunners will eat rattlesnakes for breakfast!

Strategy guru Gary Hamel put it well in an article he wrote for the *Harvard Business Review*: "Corporations around the world are reaching the limits of incrementalism. Squeezing another penny out of costs, getting product to market a few weeks earlier, responding to customers' inquiries a little bit faster, ratcheting quality up one more notch, capturing another point of market share—those are the obsessions of managers today. But pursuing incremental improvements while rivals reinvent the industry is like fiddling while Rome burns."

Hamel's message may sound overly dramatic, but we predict that it will become a watchword of the emerging millennium. In a business world overwhelmed with social and demographic change, bursting with advances in technology and science, and crowded with throngs of jostling competitors (all doing the same continuous improvement of the status quo, by the way), the winners will be those organizations that have the commitment to concentrate on breakthrough and the wherewithal to make it happen.

When a business leader says, "Well, this may be well and good for Michael Dell, but our business is different," what he or she is really saying is that the barriers that Wile E. faces are to him real, daunting, and insurmountable. The Road Runner never assumes that anything is insurmountable, which is why he breaks through. Whenever this occurs, Wile E. tries to imitate the Road Runner, but he can't. He smashes into the wall the bird has just plowed through. He lacks the imagination, courage, skills, and—most important—the faith.

Wile E. stands in the middle of the road, in front of a big sign he's painted with the words: "Stop! Bridge out!" He pushes a big screen onto the road and on it paints a scene of a canyon with a bridge which has been washed out. He then scampers to the side of the road and hides. The Road Runner approaches and, without slowing down, runs right through the screen, leaving only his silhouette behind. Wile E. looks stunned and depressed and proceeds to run toward the screen. He makes it through the screen and then falls straight down to the "canyon" floor.

What's real? What isn't? Does the canyon really exist? How about the many tunnels Wile E. has painted on a mountain face? Are they real? Yes, and no. The Road Runner never assumes obstacles are real enough to keep him from his goals. But simultaneously, and paradoxically, he *uses* the barriers to actually make the breakthroughs. That is, he turns the screen or the tunnel itself into the means for doing the extraordinary. This is something the Coyote cannot imitate, even though he too is aware of the barrier (heck, he created it). But he cannot break through it, no matter how he tries, because he's stuck in a conventional way of looking at the world. He's a prisoner of his own conventional wisdom.

Breakthrough Is the *Road*

Breakthroughs come in many forms. Some are radically new and original. Some are an adaptation of a current product or service, successfully reinvented in terms of function, attraction, or durability. However, creating or formulating a breakthrough is just the beginning. It is one step on the *road* to prosperity. What the organization *does* in the market is equally important. Even if you build the world's best mousetrap, there's no guarantee the world will beat a path to your door, no matter what Ralph Waldo Emerson thought.

Breakthrough is not about the great product whose life cycle will be short. It's about getting on the road to many great products, laying a pipeline of innovation. Being the first to come up with something radical and innovative is only half the trick. What steps and what direction you take ultimately determine the outcome. And, since most roads are neither straight nor flat, roadrunners need tenacity and adaptability to make it to the end. Sony innovated with Betamax, but Philips won the race with VHS, opening up the road by making their proprietary technology available to others. Apple innovated but then stagnated. Microsoft took over and scored. It takes doers as well as dreamers to own the road.

You won't see the Road Runner in one place for long. That means you can be sure that he won't be resting on a rock or on his laurels after a breakthrough. Persistent searches for the next breakthrough mark this bird. FedEx broke through with overnight delivery, but competitive challenges by UPS, DHL, the U.S. Postal Service, fax, and e-mail further propelled FedEx to breakthrough in the third-party logistics markets by applying its great technologies. ESPN breaks through with new product extensions—ESPN2 (for Generation X'ers), ESPN radio, Web sites like ESPN Net Sportszone (updated 1,000 times an hour), sports promotions like the ESPY awards, and—most recently—a new sports magazine to challenge the likes of *Sports Illustrated.*

> Armed with a sheet of Acme Triple-Strength Battleship Steel Armor Plate, Wile E. hides behind a rock, waiting for the Road Runner. As the Road Runner approaches, Wile E. jumps into the middle of the road, holding up the armor plate in front of him. The Road Runner runs right through the plating, making a hole with the shape of his silhouette. Wile E. looks around, then looks down at himself, and with one droopy ear, blinks and meekly walks to the side of the road, holding the plating up in front of him.

Dell Computer is a leader in the new wave: Internet breakthroughs. Building customized Web sites for corporate customers yields tighter electronic linkages and faster, highly tailored services. Internet-based sales and service software protocols allow corporate and individual customers to create and buy their computer products online and then fix them when things go wrong.

Its new "breakthrough" to prosperity is launching a huge online store that will sell over 30,000 computer and electronics products in addition to its own products. Dell's move takes its Internet expertise and expands it to include other company's products and accessories. The idea is not merely another source of revenue, but also a way to get customers and potential customers hooked to Dell's Web sites to help build PC sales and ultimately to build a brand. Currently, Internet sales at Dell are $18 million a day. Its Web sites are among the most visited sites on the Web: about 2.5 million visitors per week.

Roadrunners Make Chicken Salad out of Chicken Sh_t

The conventions that constrain coyotes are the very source of potential breakthroughs. For example, if you're a travel agency, is the rapid advent of online self-booking in air travel and lodging a barrier to prosperity? For coyote-like agencies who cling to the past, denying the inevitable, the answer is "yes!" For those who merely "improve" current processes, the answer is also "yes."

For Rosenbluth Travel, it is a resounding "No!" This already successful $3 billion global company sees breakthrough potential in developing a whole new stream of business: an entire line of new software and support services aimed at helping customers do self-bookings—even as it does regular incremental improvements in its conventional over-the-phone travel agency business. What the coyote sees as an insurmountable barrier, the roadrunner sees as a breakthrough opportunity.

The key in successful strategy is to do the unconventional today, *before* it becomes the next big thing that everyone else rushes to emulate. Do you notice that the same people rushing to mimic Dell's direct-sales, no-inventory approach in computers are the same people who derided that business model a few years ago? Even when everyone then tries to follow, you'll be way ahead of the pack. What do Nike, Dell, Schwab, Wal-Mart, CNN, and Amazon.com have in common? At their birth, they broke and rewrote industry rules, they created dominant brands, they made a ton of money for their founders, and they eventually spawned a slew of imitators trying to catch up —in the case of CNN, it took fifteen years. Oh, one other thing: Because they flouted conventional wisdom, each of these company's founders was initially labeled insane by industry pundits, analysts, competitors, and even customers.

Amazon.com is a good example. Started in a Seattle

garage in July 1995, the company had sales of half a million dollars in its first year, $16 million in 1996, and $85 million in 1997. As of May 1999, revenues were $610 million. Not bad, but from the perspective of future growth potential, it gets even better, for the market value of Amazon.com was appraised at over $22 billion. Why? Because of exceptional revenue growth without the fixed costs of stores and, even more important, because Amazon represents a new business model. The company will be selling more than just books, which means that it will effectively act as an Internet mall, accessible real-time to anyone in their pajamas sitting in front of a PC. Amazon is redefining the entire world of retailing (read, breakthrough!) and putting new pressures on existing retailers to create a new "knock your socks off" customer experience to entice people into their stores—that will require breakthrough as well.

Says founder Jeff Bezos: "Nobody sane would have predicted that we would be where we are today after a few years." If your strategy is not considered insane by traditional industry observers, you're probably still operating within the cell block of conventional wisdom.

Racing on the Lunatic Fringe

Wile E. Coyote is both dumb-founded and skeptical at the feats Road Runner performs. How can he possibly go through the "tunnel" or cross the "canyon" in midair? This is exactly the reaction that road-runner businesspeople receive from their contemporaries. When Ted Turner launched CNN and predicted that his viewership would exceed the circulation of *Time* magazine (which it has), he was considered insane by industry pundits and by entrenched competitors like the Big Three TV networks. When Debbi Fields launched Mrs. Fields Original Cookies, she was considered hopelessly naive by folks in the food service and packaged goods industry.

Turner didn't view the barriers cited by the management consultants and industry analysts as insurmountable. He was well aware of them, but ultimately he recognized they were completely bogus. He had no intention of directly challenging the Big Three TV networks with a me-too product. He had no intention of blindly following the "competitor analysis" and "market research" studies, all of which reflected the conventional wisdom of the time—and all of which turned a thumbs-down to his approach.

Instead, he looked at the trends in society and in the marketplace—all data in the public domain, by the way, nothing secret—and saw that adults were ready for more news and a richer variety of information than the half-hour, Walter Cronkite–type programming offered by the Big Three. He realized adults wanted their news and information on *their* time frame at *their* convenience—not the network's. And he realized he could deliver his product via new technologies like satellite uplinks and cable. Breakthrough!

Likewise, at a time when conventional wisdom dictated that commercial chocolate chip cookies could not be sold except in packages in supermarkets, Debbi Fields's in-your-face "street samples" ("Excuse me, sir, would you like to try this cookie free of charge?") experiences suggested to her that people would indeed pay a high-margin premium price to buy big, hot, luscious cookies sold individually in tiny, cost-efficient, conveniently located mall shops. Breakthrough!

Whenever a start-up creates a breakthrough—like a Mrs. Fields, a Nike, an ESPN, a Starbucks—good things happen. Whenever an established company does a breakthrough— like when Kinko's reinvents its business from being simply a copy center for college students to being a complete virtual office for businesspeople, or when Diebold reinvents its business from being simply a manufacturer of ATMs and safes to a provider of security products and services for electronic transactions—good things happen. When WorldCom redefines the telecom business in terms of bundled voice/video/data transmission in a high-speed, high-bandwidth medium—good things happen. When American Standard reinvents a "bathtub" to include features like Touch-Tone telephone and stereo and microprocessor control systems for TV and alarm—good things happen. When companies like Intel, Charles Schwab, Sony, Toyota, Hewlett-Packard, and Quad/Graphics continually cannibalize and abandon their successful products and come out with powerful, market-carving, next-generation sequels—good things happen.

Coyote organizations are uncomfortable with all this. They have no idea of what to make of GE Chairman Jack Welch, who told the *Wall Street Journal*: "You can't proceed in a calm, rational manner. You have to be out there on the lunatic fringe." Or when change consultant Price Pritchett writes: "Organizations need radicals, rebels and revolutionaries. People who howl at the moon."

Roadrunners understand that today's lunacy is tomorrow's conventional wisdom; today's conventional wisdom is tomorrow's historical footnote; today's fad is tomorrow's antique. They can't figure out Sun Microsystems CEO Scott McNealy, who declared: "I want Sun to be controversial. If everybody believes in your strategy, you have zero chance of profit." Roadrunners know that if coyotes understand your strategy, if they find it "reasonable," if they can predict your moves, you're tonight's dinner.

Risk Is Its Own Reward

Coyotes find it difficult to accept the new roadrunner reality. They're skeptical when Tom Peters writes "Revolutionary times call for revolutionary zeal and leaders. . . . Innovation should be your top-line obsession." And they're baffled by James Collins and Perry Porras's *Built to Last* research, which shows that the most effective long-lasting companies consistently set "Big Hairy Audacious Goals" and, in fact, sometimes go as far as to bet the company on a solid idea, like IBM with its 360 mainframe or Boeing with its 747 aircraft.

"It's all too risky," coyote managers say. So they seek the haven of what may have worked in the past or, per conventional wisdom, cling to the plan that "ought" to work, and, well . . .

Wile E. finishes paving a patch of road with "Quick Drying Cement." When he hears the familiar "Beep Beep," he hides. The Road Runner runs right through the cement, splashing it all over the hiding coyote. Wile E. begins to run after the bird, but true to its name, the cement dries, leaving Wile E. frozen in mid-run.

It didn't work before; it won't work now. Coyote organizations often seek the shelter of incrementalism because they believe it's safer, even as roadrunner competitors are reinventing the rules of the game completely. Coyotes zealously protect their current products and services because they believe it's safer to do that, even as roadrunner competitors are busy making those products and services obsolete. (As one executive told us in the midst of a complete sweep of his organization, "Yes, what I'm doing is risky, but not doing it would be riskier.") Can you imagine the Road Runner slowly, carefully, incrementally trying to wade through the glue on the road? Even at Toyota, they're saying that kaizen—continuous improvement of current processes and products—is no longer enough. As Senior Vice President Doug West explained, nonrevolutionary change makes no sense in the face of the emerging "consumer-led revolutions"—his words—going on in his business.

Mexican billionaire Alfonso Romo is galvanizing his seed company Empresa La Moderna SA, according to a *Wall Street Journal* story, to create "utopian vegetables," like non-browning lettuce and broccoli with enhanced cancer-fighting properties. "Seeds are software," says Romo. Breakthrough concept! Small wonder Monsanto (itself reinventing from a bulk chemicals company to a "life science" business) is so eager to join forces with this pathfinder.

Even as major record labels consolidate globally and stick to tried-and-true production and distribution channels, new feisty companies are fearlessly appearing on stage with little respect for conventional wisdom. As noted earlier, these companies have strange names: N2K, Headspace, Liquid Audio, and such—and they are all dedicated to the proposition that the emerging world of music is less about tangibles like audiotapes or compact disks—and more about digital intangibles called music. Creating multiple matrices of Web music sites and using technologies like MP3 data formats, these companies offer consumers increasing opportunities to sample music from an enormous inventory (much larger than in any bricks-and-mortar retailer), and then, if desired, to cut, paste, and download what they want in order to create their own customized digital product.

Poor coyotes! In their never-ending quixotic quest to eliminate risk, they sink mega-dollars into expedient mergers and acquisitions because they believe that they can simply buy market share by doubling up on the same-old-same-old or that the scale and synergies of me-too, commoditized products and services will somehow yield salvation. Sure, when companies seek judicious, cutting-edge acquisitions in order to ignite a market breakthrough—the modus operandi of companies like WorldCom, Microsoft, and Cisco Systems, for example—there's a potential for bigger, more powerful road-runners to emerge, which is why the stock market has loved them. Think of the physics: speed = mass × acceleration. But, consider also that a lot of faltering merger deals are the equivalent of two coyotes mating. They won't produce a road-runner offspring, just a bigger, heavier, more sluggish coyote.

The issue is not mergers and acquisitions. The question ought to be, do the deals prepare the participants for the Age of the Road Runner? Do they transform/ metamorphosize the participants into roadrunners? Or do they simply make the participants larger, lumpier, albeit more efficient coyotes? Most deals appear to do the latter, which is why the unbiased empirical research indicates that most of them will ultimately reduce shareholder value. As Milacron Senior Vice President Alan Shaffer says: "If two coyotes join forces to ambush a roadrunner, they usually wind up ambushing each other."

The final trump card of coyote thinking is: "Let someone else try it first, and then we'll get into it." Less risky? Hardly, because unlike the tortoise and the hare fable, roadrunners don't fall asleep or politely wait for the coyote to catch up. Besides, isn't it naive to think you can act like a coyote 99 percent of the time and then suddenly switch species to act like a roadrunner? It can't be done! This is one of the most interesting perspectives offered in the cartoons. The Road Runner roars through the tunnel, through the glue, across the bridge, and the Coyote then tries to follow him. He can't. He's encumbered by his past, his mind-set, his very being.

The Light at the End of the Tunnel

Roadrunners seek breakthroughs through the barriers that coyotes find insurmountable. They know that in terms of building corporate value and wealth, breakthroughs are less risky than coyote thinking because they yield extraordinary consequences:

- You get to define the new market, define customers' expectations in this new market, and establish yourself as "the" brand.
- You establish a legitimate monopoly, however temporary, and you get to charge a premium price in the process.
- You differentiate yourself in a marketplace filled with competitors desperate to differentiate themselves.
- You create a head-start learning infrastructure (systems, processes, technologies, databases, networks, alliances) with the capacity to improve your breakthrough radically, and make further breakthroughs, even as your competitors are desperately scampering to catch up.
- You get introduced to new niches, new ideas, new possibilities, and new alliances your strategic plan never anticipated.
- You boost the morale of your current employees and you start attracting the best and brightest talent in the labor pool.
- You wind up delighting your stakeholders with the earnings, margins, and share increases that you (humbly) declare.

Breakthrough is the road to prosperity, regardless of your size. If you're big, you can no longer coast on your name or balance sheet. As *Fortune*'s Anne Fisher wrote in describing the 1998 "Most Admired Companies" (all big ones, like Toyota and FedEx), "In addition to the great product and great marketing/financial acumen, these companies . . . also have something else: guts. Their managers are willing to take some risks so bold they may cause shareholders, stock analysts, and employees to seriously question their sanity—at least until they turn out to have been right."

Like Andrew Sather, a twenty-seven-year-old who five years ago quit the University of Wisconsin and started a business in his parents' home, building customized Web sites for a scraggle of interested individual customers. Today, via the power of word-of-mouth referrals ("check out what this kid is doing!") he's running a set of suites in San Francisco. He's the Chairman and CEO (though his first title is Creative Director) of a 100-person company called Adjacency, which builds sizzling, category-defining, "cool" corporate Web sites for global brands, like Nordstrom, Johnson Wax, Land Rover, Williams Sonoma, Virgin Entertainment, and nearly thirty other clients—including the White House. Nearly all these clients (including the White House) came to Adjacency once they saw what the company did for others.

Adjacency has reinvented the image, look, and feel of what a corporate Web site can be. No more vanilla sites with a touch of color aimed at providing some pizzazz. Adjacency's Web sites seem to live and breathe; they grab viewers, inviting their input and participation. Per Adjacency's mission, the Web sites are to be "beautifully designed, high-visibility, high-traffic Web sites . . . that inform, engage, and empower consumers."

But that's not all. Adjacency not only builds and supports the Web sites, but also runs the electronic commerce off them. Take Virgin, for example. Adjacency has full operational responsibilities for processing sales off the Virgin Web site, tying them to back-end ERP, identifying online business opportunities, and continually intervening with strategic consulting to Internet-enable the Virgin business fully. This is why Sather describes Virgin as a partner, not simply a customer. In fact, he says, "We seek long-term relationships with clients who are fully committed to exploring the possiblities of e-business with us. We do not take on short-term project work. We turn it away. We want to be the cerebellum, not a pair of wrists." This strategy has been very lucrative for Adjacency. The company has enjoyed a 300 percent growth rate over the past four years, with 30 percent average net profit. Its reputation is such that it wins contracts over logarithmically larger competitors. It's gotten to the point, in fact, that Sather no longer considers some of the traditional big marketing consultancies or advertising agencies as serious rivals.

First of all, "they don't *get* e-commerce. They see it as a peripheral event. We see it as a means to radically transform a brand and its core business processes."

Second, "we beat them on lucrative accounts not because we set out to beat them, but because we set out to do superwork. Our culture is based on no hierarchy and full meritocracy. Performance and intelligence are rewarded, not who you know or how long you've been here. So the work that people produce is fast and great. We won the 1998 Gold Clio, the most prestigious award in advertising, for the Best Web site for our work with Apple stores (see www.store.apple.com). We beat out huge companies. But their size doesn't scare us. I believe that scale doesn't create genius. In fact, scale often stifles genius."

That's a lot of confidence, and it's not unwarranted. A kid in his parents' house puts together a breakthrough Web site business that roars past the conventional efforts of big ad agencies and media empires.

Speaking of media, consider Mitch Schlimer, who started a New York City–based enterprise that breaks new ground in aiding entrepreneurs. It's called the Let's Talk Business Network, or LTBN, and it's about using media to create a *community* for entrepreneurs around the world. Schlimer points out that 99 percent of businesses are considered "small businesses" and that 80 percent of them fail in the first five years; then 80 percent of the survivors fail in the next five years. Declaring "someone has to do something about this," Schlimer launched LTBN with three compatriots in 1994 not simply as a business but as a "cause": a one-stop shopping mecca for entrepreneurs and, even more important, a place where entrepreneurs can "meet" to obtain practical advice, emotional comfort, business partnerships, and new friends. LTBN is a hodgepodge of integrated activities and products, like the nationwide, acclaimed *Let's Talk Business* call-in radio show (which is also beamed and archived online), the *Let's Talk Business* cable network, the *www.LTBN.com* interactive community Web site, the online LTBN University (a Web-based

teleconference format to teach subjects that will support entrepreneurs), the *Ultimate Mastermind* newsletter, and as-
sorted products like the *Road to Success* audiotape series.

But the LTBN concept goes even further. Schlimer's vision
is to make the LTBN model easily replicable so that he can
perpetually spin it off to local communities of interested entrepreneurs. He sees a myriad of networked LTBN chapters
around the world providing customized support services to
their local members. He's shooting for a thousand LTBNs in
ten years. Already LTBN has been licensed in Washington,
D.C., and Vancouver, British Columbia. To some extent,
Schlimer's concept looks like an NBC network providing
local affiliates with product. But, interestingly, his model is
more akin to Kinko's, which joint-partners with and co-owns
hundreds of individual stores around the world and provides
them with corporate guidance, central databases, and ongoing resources. Either way, Schlimer's dream of uniting a
world community of entrepreneurs is already having an impact, and it's not surprising why sales have been growing 100
to 200 percent annually.

Then there's Robert Winquist, CEO of Vending Supply,
Inc. based in Reno, Nevada. This tiny company, which didn't
even exist until 1995, is already one of the most dominant
players in the $60 million machine-vended children's stickers
business. (If you don't know what the children's stickers
business is, talk to some kids in the five- to twelve-year-old
range. They devour these stickers at 50 cents a pop and paste
them on everything from schoolbooks to skateboards.)
Vending Supply has turned the entire industry upside down,
explains Winquist: "The big guys used to dominate—but
their products were banal—the stickers were dull, uninteresting images—little flowers, fish, airplanes, that sort of
thing. So, what we did was hang out with kids, and we radically improved the product. We launched Scratch 'n' Sniff
Roses, black shark-tooth smileys, alien heads, and tie-dye
hippie VW microbuses.

"We also created new patterns and new production techniques to generate images with even wilder colors and hues. We also improved our service to the vendors themselves, and did something unthinkable in this business—we offered a 100 percent refund policy.

"What's interesting," continues Winquist, "is that we were so successful that the big-bulk vending suppliers got interested in the sticker business. So they bought a bunch of small companies and licenses, and they released a ton of new products priced cheaper than ours. But they forgot one little thing—the kids have to like the products. And they didn't!" BREAKTHROUGH!

Prosperity Is Never Final

One final note. In the cartoons, you can bet that the Road Runner never assumes that one breakthrough will ensure permanent success. There's always tomorrow, and Wile E. will be skulking around with some new scheme, and there'll be some new contraption to "Beep Beep" through. Without eternal vigilance, and without a perpetual commitment to breakthrough, the Road Runner might be caught. Like Mrs. Fields Original Cookies, for example, after it was sold to Capricorn Investors. It remains a viable business, but the lack of further breakthroughs has diminished much of its brand luster and financial sheen; it's now one of many players in the retail cookie business. In contrast, roadrunner companies like Dell, Microsoft, FedEx, Metamor Worldwide, America Online, ESPN, Kinko's, and Rosenbluth, and thousands of little but powerful shops like Vending Supply, Inc., Colwick Travels, and Retirement Advisors of America—are roadrunner-like, racing down a continuous breakthrough ROAD. They never stop, which is why their ticket is to prosperity.

Perpetual movement. Perpetual innovation. Perpetual restlessness. Perpetual energy. Perpetual confidence about doing the so-called impossible. That's what describes the roadrunner companies, and their leaders. Coyote competitors are left scratching their heads or licking their wounds.

Wile E. pours glue over a large portion of the road (he just won't give up on this idea). He grabs a stick of dynamite and gets ready to throw it. He hears the "Beep Beep," and he lights the dynamite. The Road Runner runs right through the glue, causing a major splash, covering his adversary. Wile E. tries to throw the dynamite, but he can't because it's glued to one of his hands. As he tries to pull the stick of dynamite off his hand, he simply succeeds in getting *both* his hands and his feet stuck to it. He then creeps-hops his body to the edge of the cliff overlooking a river and jumps off. But just before he hits the water—BOOM! His charred remains barely make a ripple in the water.

The Breakthrough Roadrunner Leader

When leadership expert Warren Bennis was asked the single most challenging attribute for contemporary leaders to demonstrate, his answer: "Courage!" The nature of organizations, with their propensity for conformity and their aversion to dissonance and disorder, makes bravery arduous to marshal. But roadrunner leaders invariably manage to bring courage to the table. Are they always confident and self-assured? Of course not! Sometimes, courageous courses are taken with a stomach-in-your-throat anxiety, but they *are* taken.

Breakthrough roadrunner leaders also seek out people doing new and different things in order to provide them support, eliminate obstacles, and ensuring that their different drumbeat always keeps them marching. Breakthrough leaders often take the heat for these mavericks. They are tolerant of their eccentricities, choosing to pay attention to their results more than their style, their special gifts over their odd ways. Roadrunners know that strong substance is more crucial than approval and affability.

Roadrunner leaders set big goals and then communicate a deep belief in their associates to achieve them. Big goals are fresh birdseed to roadrunners. Thriving on pushing-the-limits aims, they respond to leaders who share their intoxication with challenge. Affirmed by a leader's belief in them, they dig even deeper into the groundwater of determination, producing award-winning, record-breaking performance.

BIRDSEED

- Take a hard look at your team's or organization's vision and strategy. Do words like *audacious, revolutionary*, or *changing the rules of the industry* describe them? Or would customers (ask them!) say that you were simply imitations of your competitors?
- Go for the lunatic fringe. If your competitors aren't saying you're crazy, if they aren't asking "What the hell are those people (you!) doing?" you're probably not doing anything breakthrough; you're just one of the predictable pack.
- Think *big*. Focus on rewriting the rules of the game. Yes, of course, do incrementalism—always improving your current products, services, and processes. But know that the in-

cremental approach is simply the road to surviving. To get on the road to thriving, get people on your staff to think breakthrough when they approach things like business development, product enhancement, alliances, cycle time reduction, and customer service.

- Don't accept any barrier as being real. Whether it's how you deal with suppliers, or how you deal with employees, or how you do your capital budgeting, or where you invest those dollars—don't let conventional wisdom and tradition keep you trapped.
- Remember that breakthrough is a perpetual process. There's no such thing as the grand-slam home run followed by eternal bliss. Perpetual vigilance, perpetual movement, perpetual evolution, perpetual breakthrough—that's the road to sustainable competitive advantage.

Tail Feathers: A Maverick in Motion

••

Glenn Kravitz, forty-seven years old, sits alone in his home office in Los Angeles. He's been on the phones since 6:00 A.M., beginning another fourteen-hour day in his quest toward making CalmSoft a success. He is living the reality of an Internet start-up. For every Bill Gates and Michael Dell, there are umpteen failures. Glenn knows this, but it hasn't dissuaded him. He's committed to a unique vision, and he's prepared to go through the pain to achieve it.

In 1996, Dr. Mory Framer approached Glenn with an intriguing proposition. Mory's company, the Los Angeles–based Barrington Clinic, provided trauma response and medical-legal evaluation to its clients, which were companies seeking protection against questionable workers' compensation claims and civil lawsuits. Over the years, Mory had developed very specific criteria that would, with extraordinary accuracy, predict which employees were likely to exhibit productivity declines and absenteeism, file grievances, or submit workers' compensation claims. Mory's research had shown that his predictive model could help a company help individual employees before their problems became acute and save the company literally millions of dollars. To apply his model, he also developed a rudimentary software program called C.A.L.M. (Comprehensive Analysis for Loss Management).

Mory's proposal to Glenn was twofold: Help me build a better C.A.L.M. product, and help me build a company around C.A.L.M. Become a 50 percent partner with me. After several months of thought, anxiety, and research, Glenn agreed. He closed down his marketing business and shrunk his pool supply company, Crystal Pool, to a simple order-taking shell. While his fiancée (now wife) remained in San Francisco, he moved to Los Angeles in order to work closely with Mory.

Glenn threw body and soul into the quintessential entrepreneur's dream: the Internet start-up. In this case: a company named Calm-Soft. While "Internet start-up" may sound "cool," the day-to-day reality is an incessant grind: setting up a legal business entity, conducting due diligence and industry analyses, building an active board, contacting potential customers and distributors, developing technical partnerships to upgrade the software, building a prototype product, formulating a business plan to raise capital, seeking investors, seeking top people to form a management team, preparing a sales and marketing effort. The tasks went on and on and on and on.

What's it like giving up everything in order to start a high-risk venture, we asked him. Here's what Glenn e-mailed us back:

- You must have a burning desire and strong belief in your proposed business.
- You must be willing to risk it all. (Savings and the scaled-back Crystal Pool generated enough income to help fund CalmSoft and put food on the table, with very little left over.)
- You must dedicate 110 percent of your time to stay focused on developing the business.
- You must embrace small successes on the road to bigger things.
- It helps to have an extremely supportive significant other.
- It helps to have a fallback position (in this case, Crystal Pool) in the event of failure.
- You must be totally committed, highly motivated, persistent, and tenacious.

For the last two years, Glenn has positioned CalmSoft to take off as an Internet-based application service provider that will identify the productivity and health declines of employees and then take follow-up intervening actions. The company will be able to provide its clients with a "visual and statistical snapshot of high-risk behavior, a virtual MRI, so to speak," Glenn says. "Business experience losses in the tens of billions of dollars annually due to employee productivity declines, civil lawsuits, and workers' compensation claims. Our products can make a huge dent in that loss spiral. That's our vision."

Is the work over? Hardly. We write this passage in March 1999. The grind of selling the business plans to venture capitalists, launching a finished product, building a customer base, and forming a top-level management team are still pressing concerns. But by the time you read this, Glenn Kravitz is certain that CalmSoft will not be one of those many great ideas that simply died for lack of execution. In fact, he has projected that CalmSoft will be a $100 to $200 million company in five to seven years.

We'll see if Glenn's predictions come through. But we'll put our money on him, based on his response to one of our questions: How do you keep from getting depressed and burnt out? "Ah," he replied, "the secret is that with CalmSoft, I am in control of my own destiny and the destiny of my company. I believe strongly that what I'm doing is a good thing for people. I believe I can make a significant contribution to the world and make some money out of it. That's what gives me the energy and inspiration to go on."

He has just described the fuel that powers roadrunners and their enterprises, regardless of whether or not they're start-ups. We'll bet on that.

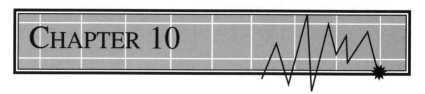

CHAPTER 10

Giggles
The Last Word Is . . . Laughter

The desert is a harsh, unforgiving environment. On the surface, it is certainly not one that appears conducive to laughter and gaiety. Yet the Road Runner always seems to be happy. Is that the consequence of his success—or the cause?

A roadrunner thrives in the furnace-like heat of the desert. And under his colorful feathered exterior is a coarse, fur-like down that enables him to endure the extreme cold of desert nights. Though a roadrunner will drink water whenever available, he can go for long periods without it. His diet ranges from bread crumbs and watermelon rind to such exotica as scorpions, tarantulas, snakes, bumblebees, and horned toads. In short, he has the goods to thrive on whatever gets tossed, dropped, or forced on him.

The global marketplace is a lot like the desert. It can be depressing or invigorating, bleak or beautiful, depending on whether you approach it like the Coyote or the Road Runner. Roadrunners do more than adapt. They face adversity with a spirited, playful attitude. In the early days of California, pioneers often saw roadrunners racing their stagecoaches. As cars appeared in the early 1900s, goggle-eyed travelers used to bet on how fast these odd birds could run alongside their noisy vehicles. In Arizona, a roadrunner took up residence in a roadside telephone booth, allowing locals to stroke his head while they made phone calls. Roadrunners have been known to move into hen houses, adjusting easily to the chickens' banter and diet.

Our little cartoon Road Runner is always puckish, smiling, and joyful. He's having fun! If the arena is the desert, place your bets on the roadrunner and follow his lead to fun and laughter. Why fun? Why laughter? Try the following mental mixture and see what conclusion you draw.

- Ninety-six percent of the executives in an Accountemps survey believed that people with a sense of humor do better at their jobs than those who have little or no sense of humor.
- *USA Today* reports that while the average workweek is down from 42.8 hours in 1948 to 39.5 hours today, people feel more work-related stress. New technology has created a much faster paced workweek.
- In the nine months following a workshop on Fun at Work at Digital Equipment Corporation, twenty middle managers increased their productivity by 15 percent and reduced their sick days by half.
- Employees from the Colorado Health Sciences Center in Denver who viewed humorous training films and attended fun workshops showed a 25 percent decrease in downtime and a 60 percent increase in job satisfaction.
- Sixty percent of those queried in a major research study said they felt stressed because they had less time for leisure. Forty-four percent confessed that, given the choice, they'd rather have more free time than more money.

Smart organizations are learning what the Road Runner has always known: Laughter pays! The relationship between fun and productivity has been demonstrated in numerous studies. Roadrunner organizations hire fun-loving people and create an environment in which people take their work seriously, but not themselves.

Sun Microsystems CEO Scott McNealy encourages Sun employees to "work hard, play hard." Sun's corporate environment is arranged into "campuses" that are colorful and relaxed, complete with on-site gymnasiums and Ping-Pong rooms. Employees form sports teams that play each other during lunch hours: soccer, football, volleyball, and hockey (McNealy's passion). As one Sun employee explains, this atmosphere not only relieves stress and breaks up long days, but helps employees build close relationships that carry into the business side.

An article in *Esquire* magazine on Richard Branson, the extraordinary CEO of the Virgin Atlantic empire, concluded that there were two traits that explained his remarkable successes. One, "he hates to lose." The second: "He loves fun." Specifically: "He is the chief funmeister, taking out 350 of his staff while he is in the United States. Glass and cigarette in hand, he closes down more than one bar a night three nights in a row and comes home at dawn, his pockets stuffed with notes and ideas. Iron men have this constitution and freak energy so that they can get up the next morning ready to deal and take over without twisters in their brains."

And what businessperson does Branson admire? Herb Kelleher! "Kelleher once invited Branson to meet him on one of his planes. When Branson boarded, he pulled down one of the overhead compartments and a flight attendant popped out; then girls popped out of all the racks and said 'Hello, Richard!' Now that is his kind of executive."

Roadrunner Herb Kelleher, Chairman of Southwest Airlines, says, "I want flying to be a helluva lot of fun. We want people who can do things well with laughter and grace." *Fortune* magazine nicknamed Kelleher "The High Priest of Ha Ha" and in the same breath acknowledged that his wacky leadership reigned over the only U.S. airline to have made money every year since 1973, up 300 percent since 1990, with the lowest turnover, highest customer service ratings, best safety record and the only airline to win the industry's "Triple Crown" (best baggage handling, best on-time performance, and lowest number of customer complaints).

Laughing All the Way to the Bank

In mid-1999, Oren addressed the top ninety managers of Blue Cross/Blue Shield of South Carolina. In the violently competitive world in which Blue Cross operates, this particular $1.3 billion company is a proven winner, enjoying an average 17 percent annual growth rate. The "South Carolina" moniker is a bit misleading because the company not only provides health insurance in South Carolina, but also processes up to 82 percent of government health claims for military and retired military persons across the entire country. Further, the company is the largest processor of Medicare claims in the United States. The company's data center, rated as one of the top 25 worldwide by IBM, handled 2.4 billion online transactions and processed 72 million health claims in 1998.

In preparing for his presentation, Oren spoke with CEO Ed Sellers. With great pride, Ed ticked off the financial and market successes of his company. But what was striking was a word he used a dozen times: *fun*. Ed's perspective is that fun is a crucial driver, not merely for spirit and morale, but for the kind of personal commitment and aggressive risks to which his managers must commit in order to maintain the company's real growth. During the meeting, Oren witnessed that the audio of fun matched the video of fun. There was a sparkling mixture of easygoing laughter and extraordinary focus, confident calmness and profound discipline, pride in achievement and a sense of optimistic urgency to improve. Even without the traditional "fun" events (golf and music, which would occur later), the entire meeting reeked of fun.

Look at the Wile E. Coyote–Road Runner cartoons, and

one thing stands out as a constant. The Road Runner is *always* smiling, and the Coyote is *always* showing some form of anxiety and tension—frowning, teeth-gritting, growling. When Wile E. attempts to smile, it's more a sneer or smirk as he contemplates how his latest brilliant scheme will finally trap the dumb, weird-looking bird.

Isn't it the Coyote demeanor that we have traditionally expected from "professional" managers? Grim, unemotional, analytical, detached. Expressionless figures in drab coats and ties (few women allowed in), sitting woodenly around a mahogany conference table, watching dull graphs embedded in uninspiring presentations.

Contrast this with the smile of the Road Runner. His smile suggests exuberance, irreverence, joy, exultation, delight, fun. If a bird could giggle, the Road Runner would. There is a childlike not childish gaiety in everything he does. Indeed, the smile is so crucial to the persona of the Road Runner that the only sound he makes—in fact, the only dialogue spoken in all the cartoons—is his comical "Beep Beep."

Road Signs of the Times

In the emerging Age of the Road Runner, roadrunner-like smiles will be both the sign and the spark of energized teamwork and can-do optimism. Take a look at three revealing quotes from a recent issue of Delta Airlines' *Sky* magazine:

Jonathan Yardley, a Pulitzer Prize–winning book critic, wrote this about what makes basketball superstar Michael Jordan heroic: "His insatiable zest for competition and the pure, irresistible joy he radiates as he engages in it."

A.M. "Tonto" Coleman, a former commissioner of the NCAA Southeast Conference, said: "I turn to the front pages of my newspaper to read about men's [aka people's] failures. I turn to the sports pages to read about their triumphs."

Then, Random House editor Elizabeth Rapoport wrote that the real virtues of sports are "teamwork, discipline, confidence, and joy."

Consider: Business is often analogized with sports. Think about these words: *zest, pure irresistible joy, triumph*; and—from Rapoport's last word—*joy*. The implications boil down to this: If you were seeing a Road Runner cartoon for the first time, on whom would you put your bet—the character who bursts with zest, pure irresistible joy, and a triumphant spirit, or his adversary, who possesses none of these attributes? If you're a customer, where do you think the most interesting, cutting-edge products and services will come from? With which vendor will you have the most pleasurable experiences—the grim, meticulous, highly focused coyote, or the laughing, irreverent, highly focused Road Runner? And if you're an investor, where do you think the sizzling ideas of the future are going to come from and where are you going to plunk down your money—with the ultra-serious, ultra-disciplined coyote, or with the equally disciplined but ultra-smiling Road Runner?

Smiles and discipline, laughs and focus, giggles and results, high performance and hee-haw. Who's to say these concepts are mutually exclusive? As a matter of fact, they belong together: Reread Yardley's and Rapoport's statements above. The successful start-ups, the fast-growing businesses are populated by people who laugh, jump with excitement, and sleep under their desks after putting in twenty-five-hour days. And reinvigorated businesses, like Unisys, will be infused with a similar spirit—if they're lucky.

The Road Runner teaches us something else: He takes his mission very seriously, but he doesn't take anything or anyone else seriously. Perhaps he realizes both birds and humans are here for such a short time, so why sweat the small stuff when in the big scheme, it's all small stuff. Few people lament on their deathbed that they wished they'd spent more time at the office. The Road Runner teaches us the value of laughing at a vice president's pomposity or our own mistakes.

The Road Runner is amused at the entire theater in which he operates. He knows exactly what the Coyote is trying to do and seems to enjoy the process. Sometimes, we see him standing on a boulder or ledge *above* the Coyote, watching—with a confident, serene smile—the Coyote prepare his latest contraption. Occasionally he comes even closer.

The Road Runner is zooming down the road. Wile E. stands behind a rock next to the road, holding a trash can lid. As the Road Runner approaches, Wile E. suddenly holds the lid out to block his way. The Road Runner skids to a complete stop. Wile E. blinks his eyes; the Road Runner blinks back and sticks his tongue out, and with a "Beep Beep" he turns around and speeds off. Wile E. slams the trash can lid to the ground and gets ready to run after the Road Runner. The Road Runner comes right back, picks up the lid, and holds it up so that Wile E. smashes right into it. The Road Runner sticks his tongue out again, Beeps, and runs on.

The Road Runner's sense of confidence and awareness gives further fuel to his sense of amusement. The Road Runner is so tuned into the desert drama of coyote vs. roadrunner that he scoffs at the Coyote's efforts and delightedly turns the tables on him. We see a coyote-launched boulder hurtling down the mountain on a beeline for the Road Runner, who is zooming up the same path. We grow increasingly nervous about the inevitable collision as the screen switches back and forth between a boulder accelerating down and a bird accelerating up. We are discomfited by the Road Runner's steady smile as he charges up. And then, at the last second, when the Road Runner suddenly avoids the boulder by making a 90 degree turn into a side road, we realize he knew about the alternative path all along and was probably chuckling at our nervousness as well.

Even weirder is the spectacle of a truck roaring out of a tunnel, flattening the Coyote, who thought he was chasing the Road Runner. It turns out the driver of the truck is the Road Runner himself, looking back with a big smile as "The End" flashes on the screen.

> Wile E. has cross-dressed, wearing a blond wig, makeup, green blouse, white skirt, and high-heeled shoes. He's got two suitcases next to him, one saying "Old Virginny or bust." Wile E. makes hitchhiking motions, with his other hand on his hip, shaking his rear, trying to look sexy. The Road Runner comes by and knocks the coyote up into the air. When Wile E. comes down, he looks up to see the Road Runner run back to him wearing a blond wig and holding a sign saying "I've already got a date."

The Road Runner's attitude and antics raise some very important questions: Why should work be so grim? Why should "professionalism" be equated with seriousness? Why are jobs joyless? Why are things like smiles and fun considered frivolous, silly, unimportant, "soft"—even worthless? The Road Runner challenges us to rethink our premises. Before the emergence of the industrial age, work and nonwork were indistinguishable. Life was a constant blend of both. And it was often hard, often unpleasant. The industrial age forced people to compartmentalize their lives. Work became distinct from nonwork; managers became distinct from nonmanagers; line from staff; function from function.

Work into Play

Today, in the post-industrial information age, the old categories and boundaries are blurring. In the Age of the Road Runner, they will melt together. As we're already seeing, ideas like nine to five, workweek vs. weekend, home vs. office (as opposed to home in the office), and work vs. retirement (as opposed to constant learning and development) are already challenged. Work is again indivisible from life, not a separate part of it. It's like cows grazing rather than taking three separate meals, but people will have their say about when and where they'll graze—this week I'll work on our project Monday from 8:00 A.M. to 10:00 P.M. in the office, on Tuesday I'll work on the project at home, and I think I'll go skiing with my family on Wednesday. Even more important, unlike in the pre-industrial era, work now has the potential of being more meaningful, uplifting, and enjoyable.

That's what the Road Runner is saying. If work is now an ongoing, integral part of life, there's one last artificial distinction to demolish: work vs. play. And that's how the Road Runner lives his life. He knows there are dangers, he knows he's got a relentless competitor, and thus he knows there's a lot of hard, creative work to do—but he's going to make sure he enjoys the heck out of it.

Compare the Coyote and Road Runner: Who looks gaunt and miserable; who looks healthy and happy? Who's perpetually frustrated, and who's loving the process? Who's a constant failure, and who's the success?

Wile E. is on a ledge winding up the propeller of a small toy airplane. In the pilot seat is a grenade. The Road Runner runs by and Wile E. lets go of the propeller. But only the propeller goes, leaving the rest of the plane. Realizing the flaw, the Coyote picks up the toy plane and hurls it at the Road Runner. But the grenade falls out. Thinking he has averted danger, Wile E. wipes his brow only then to see the grenade on his left. Boom!

If all this sounds far-fetched, consider: How often have we all walked into an establishment that reeks of coyote—no smiles, a prevalence of formality and anxiety, an air of secrecy and intimidation, politics and gamesmanship? How often have we attended coyote meetings in those establishments—stiff-jawed, rigid-bodied, mind-numbing? Regardless of the company's numbers today, how confident are we about its prospects tomorrow?

Consider a senior management meeting we attended. The managers were addressing a couple of pressing problems. One: The company was very slow to get new product out of the pipeline, meaning it was always playing catch-up with fleeter competitors. Two: According to the CEO, the products that were being churned out were obviously flawed in some way, as evidenced by several institutional customers that had failed to renew their orders. The results were plain: revenues down, market share down, gross margins down. On the flip side, costs were up, especially operating expenses as a percentage of revenue, which was showing a steep upturn on the graph.

The problems were urgent; no simple solutions were apparent. Yet the managers' doings would have made Wile E.

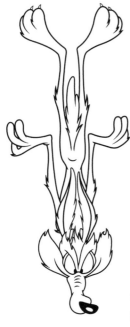

Coyote proud. One by one, they buried each other with transparencies filled with complicated numbers and graphs. Each unit head got up and gave his or her self-serving spin, assaulting the rest of the group with yet more incomprehensible data, more paper, and, periodically, unintelligible terminology familiar only to the functionary making the presentation. A consultant added fuel to the fire with a brief academic discourse on the impact of macroeconomics on marketing policy.

Here were nine men and women sitting semi-glassy-eyed, dutifully shuffling through each report, looking at transparencies filled alternatively with simple truisms ("Key Priority: Increase Market Share") or with hyper-complicated, nearly illegible charts and graphs, and only occasionally raising a polite softball sort of general query. Pure Wile E.

It's difficult to describe the effect of a couple hours of this monotonous torture, but words like *numbing* and *spiritless* suffice. After a mesmerizing three hours, everyone got up, made some parting bland small talk, and scattered. The CEO knew—nothing was going to get done to solve the problems. There was absolutely no sense of urgency, focus, agreement on priorities, commitment to specific goals—and no fun, no spirit, no eagerness to move forward, no smiles, no joy!

Compare this to Jeff Taylor's Monday Morning Unplugged session. Taylor is the founder of Monster Board, a subsidiary of TMP Worldwide and a leading career hub on the Web. Taylor uses Tinker Toys, storytelling, and "lessons learned" for his agenda-less meeting. His rationale? "Because we can sometimes take ourselves too seriously. This type of meeting allows for a moment of foolishness in a high-pressure environment. The beauty of this playtime is that everyone takes a risk and everyone learns something."

Out of the Rut

Unfortunately, in business, many of us fall into the coyote rut. Customers and employees may be unhappy, suppliers and other partners may be upset, and investors may be alarmed, but within the cool comfort of our offices, we immerse ourselves in endless analysis of printouts, reports, presentations, statistics, and surveys. We spend hours listening to ourselves analyzing and debating the merits of trifling details in mind-numbing meetings. At our desks we read reams of paper and scrolls of electronic data that gain us nothing more than a splitting headache.

We hire consultants and in-house experts who deluge us with yet more of the same. Every day we faithfully sift through mounds of voice mail and e-mail that reiterate the flood of data we've already gone though. We stay more attuned to the needs and nuances of our bosses than the marketplace. These obsessive activities not only keep us separate from our real business, but they kill our spirit, our joy, our laughter. Thus they smother any sense of creative daring and gung ho excitement about what might be possible.

Remember the scene in the comedy film *Big*, where Tom Hanks, as a thirteen-year-old trapped in the body of an adult, is sitting in a management meeting at a toy company? A pretentious executive in his thirties, promoting a proposed new toy, is presenting a tedious marketing analysis filled with charts and MBA jargon. After a few minutes, a blank Tom Hanks raises his hand and says simply, "I don't get it." The executive is annoyed and condescendingly summarizes his position. "I still don't get it," Hanks says, pointing to the toy in question.

"That's not fun!" The CEO suddenly perks up and beams. He knows that he's been bored by the babble he's been hearing, but he hasn't been able to figure out exactly why. After all, isn't this the way management meetings are supposed to be run? Suddenly, Tom Hanks's words have made it obvious the emperor has no clothes. Hanks had cut through the "coyote-speak"; the product was simply "not fun."

The Road Runner is zooming along and passes a manhole cover. Wile E., hiding underneath, lifts up the cover with his head and, aiming a gun at the bird, fires a shot at him. The bullet gradually catches up with the Road Runner, who turns around, looks at the bullet, smiles, sticks out his tongue, "Beep Beeps," and accelerates off. The bullet, still traveling, then stops itself, expels a bunch of "!!s" and "??s" out of itself as if saying "what the hell's going on?" and simply drops to the road. Wile E. runs up, picks up the bullet, looks at it and . . . kaboom.

As the Road Runner knows, anything is possible in a world that you don't take seriously, even the seemingly impossible, if you approach it with laughter. When it comes to thriving in the Age of the Road Runner, laughter is your trump card, the way you'll attract and retain roadrunners for your organization. The more grim, buttoned-down, unsmiling, and sterile the environment, the less attractive it is to great players who know they can get work elsewhere. Work hard, play hard when you're on the job. Contribute, participate, collaborate, have a sense of humor. Create, serve, and laugh. Companies like the superlative Southwest Airlines make a fetish out of fostering a fun environment, which is why they're overwhelmed with high-end applications every time they have a job opening. And in 1998, 140,000 people applied for 4,900 positions.

Laughing Leaders

"The brain is a wonderful organ," wrote Robert Frost. "It starts working the moment you get up in the morning and does not stop until you get to the office." Roadrunner leaders want brain power all day long. They know laughter is not only the best medicine; it is the master key to high performance.

Roadrunner leaders don't just allow fun; they *are* fun. Laughing is no pretending matter . . . it is real and unbridled. These leaders don't snicker; they giggle! Remember giggling? That uncontrollable, can't stop, "die laughing" you did in study hall under the monitor's disapproving stare? That's Herb Kelleher in a meeting. He giggles!

Kelleher has been known to go to board meetings in jeans and a sweatshirt. He's appeared at employee gatherings and press conferences dressed as Elvis, General Patton, and Corporal Klinger. Southwest ads show Kelleher with a "Born to Ship" or "Still Nuts After All These years" tattoo on his arm. He is the company's premier prankster, who hides in the overhead bins to scare passengers as they board a plane on Halloween. Kelleher's not the only one. Multibillionaire Warren Buffett in a recent *Fortune* magazine article said, "I tap dance to work, and when I get there I think I'm supposed to lie on my back and paint the ceiling." When asked when he planned to retire, the nearly seventy-year-old Buffett replied, "I plan to retire five years after I die. And I've given my board a Ouija board so we can communicate!" That's a roadrunner with a sense of humor!

Laughing roadrunner leaders use humor in stressful situations . . . particularly making themselves the target of the humor. Avis Rent-A-Car, under the granddaddy of all roadrunners, Robert Townsend, proudly admitted they were "Number 2 . . . and trying harder." Ross Perot would frequently respond, "I'm all ears," poking fun at his obvious exaggerated facial feature. When a reporter asked Ronald Reagan about what happened in a particular meeting, Reagan responded, "I don't know. I was asleep!"

You can't have spontaneous perpetual creativity and originality without a playful environment. Innovation is not something that is seriously, linearly planned—witness the travails of Wile E. And it's certainly not something driven by a small cadre of degree-studded serious individuals.

Roadrunner leaders also know that attracting and retaining the best people is a key competitive issue. Ernst & Young's Center for Business Innovation did a study of 275 portfolio leaders. They found that investor decisions are a "surprising" 35 percent driven by nonfinancial factors, including the "ability to attract and retain" talented employees, which ranked fifth among thirty-nine such factors investors use in picking stocks, right behind strategy execution, management credibility, quality of strategy, and innovativeness.

Roadrunner leaders want the most talented and the most fun people. They know a laughing environment is especially key to attracting and retaining the ultra-mobile, technologically savvy, self-reliant, entrepreneurially oriented Generation X and Y crowd (both as employees and customers). A cover of *Fortune* magazine featured a twenty-nine-year-old man with a parrot on his head. The title blares "Yo, Corporate America!" and went on to say that in addition to good compensation, this guy wanted "a cappuccino machine—oh, and I'm bringing my bird to work. I'm the New Organization Man. You need me."

This extends even to attracting roadrunner executives. There's a trend emerging—senior people leaving big corporations to head little start-ups for a lot less pay. Sure, the potential payoff vis-à-vis stock options is huge, but the real allure was expressed by David Dornan, who left the presidency of Pacific Bell to head up a little Internet information provider called PointCast: "I thought this would be fun." After Pacific Bell was acquired by SBC Communications, Dornan's career was solid, but he simply didn't want to go through the inevitable political and bureaucratic grind.

We don't believe the issue is big company vs. small company. The real question is whether it's time to bail from coyote life. A lot of talented executives—and talented employees—are starting to say yes. The laughing roadrunner leader knows that the key to stopping the loss of the best is to keep the grass as green on the organizations' side of the fence as it appears on the other.

"I thought this would be fun"—this is the password of our times. Fun = recreation, which means re-create (re-creation). The Road Runner makes the whole serious scene of him against Wile E. a playful environment, ensuring that his responses are creative and power-full . . . and he flourishes.

You are nearing the end of a book about the emerging Age of the Road Runner and what it will take to thrive in this brand-new terrain. We hope you have enjoyed and benefited from our story. We look forward to seeing you and your organization as new, powerful roadrunners. In the spirit of compassion, before we go to our final Tail Feathers, let's give a hand to poor ol' Wile E.

We see several boxes, two labeled "Acme Handle Bars" and "One Acme Jet Motor." Next, we see Wile E. straddling a jet motor holding on to handle bars with a devious look on his face. The Road Runner runs past. Wile E. switches on the motor and blasts away. Wile E. soon has trouble staying on, but finally gets all the way on. What follows is a long chase scene with the Coyote leaning forward, ears back, wearing a hungry look. The two get to the proverbial cliff and we watch Wile E. negotiating curve after curve and gaining. But as he gets into the Road Runner's dust, he misses a curve and flies off into midair. Still floating, Wile E. turns the jet engine off and turns around scratching his head. The Coyote floats almost to the other side of the ravine, where the Road Runner is standing on the ledge. The Road Runner Beeps and points down. Wile E. looks down, then back at the viewer, eyes wide, ears drooping. As gravity pulls him to the canyon floor, Wile E. holds up a sign which reads: "How about ending this cartoon before I hit?" He lets go of the sign and holds up another which reads, "Thank you."

Thank you for joining us on this trip!

BIRDSEED

- Put out bowls of fun candy at meetings . . . like jelly beans, M&M's, or valentine hearts with sayings.
- Open the draperies, install more windows, go outside for meetings. Place a lot of funny art or posters in your work area . . . and change it often.
- Put fun in your vision statement. Make fun one of the company values.
- Put up a graffiti wall in public areas and include crayons for doodling.
- Celebrate the company's history with photos and memorabilia. At Southwest Airlines headquarters, the People University decorates the hallways with mementos from Southwest's history and gets employees to contribute missing items. They also make a sense of humor one of their criteria for hiring.
- Turn your suggestion box and company newsletter into a big deal with a focus on fun. Play music in public areas. And get employee input on type of music. Get rid of all elevator music. Go for ragtime, jazz, marching bands, anything happy.
- Celebrate, celebrate, celebrate. Find occasions to wear costumes, like Halloween, April Fool's Day, Fourth of July, Remembrance Day. Find fun ways to celebrate birthdays. Hold an annual "baby day" when associates are encouraged to bring in babies and toddlers.
- Turn employee orientation into a unique, fun experience, like a scavenger hunt. Turn your annual "state of the organization" meeting into something festive. Instead of the usual boring department reports, require each department to present their year as a skit.
- Link associate recognition with humor. Instead of awarding a gold watch, consider a large comic book collection or the complete Dr. Seuss books.

Tail Feathers: A Road Runner with Flair

Alan Shaffer, Group Vice President of Cincinnati-based Milacron's Industrial Products division, comes on stage dressed like John Belushi in his 1980 movie *The Blues Brothers*: Black shirt, black slacks, black tie, black jacket, black fedora, black sunglasses. Five hundred sales and management folks at the December 1998 corporate retreat have just viewed *The Business Brothers*—Alan's spoof of Belushi's hit featuring a hilarious but purposeful mission for the brothers to capture a lucrative new market: small machine shops.

Now flash back to 1994. In that year's parody of the movie *Ghostbusters*, Shaffer and two other vice presidents were "Paradigm Busters" in an elaborate plot to kill the ghosts of tradition that insisted that Milacron only sold cutting-tool products. Instead, Alan's goal was to open up the Milacron sales paradigm to include new cutting-*fluid* products and a full array of high-end, high-margin tool and chemical management services wrapped around them. "Unheard of in the industry, but a very big deal," Shaffer says. "It's like Gillette selling shaving cream with the razor blades." In both the 1994 and 1998 meetings, Alan's productions had a compelling breakthrough message—accompanied by rock bands, adjunct theatrical skits, comedy presentations, laser guns, fog machines, explosives, and general madness.

Do you get the sense that Alan Shaffer might be a bit of a lunatic? And do you also get the sense that over the past eight years, he has grown his business eightfold—from $100 million to $800 million annually? That every year has seen record sales and earnings? That while industrial products were 12 percent of Milacron's business in 1992, they're nearly half of it now?

Alan Shaffer has been with Milacron his entire career, twenty-six years. And in that time, he's created so many shock waves and ruffled so many feathers that, well, he's been constantly promoted to more challenging assignments. What else do you do with a roadrunner, unless you're a hopeless coyote organization—which Milacron isn't. Alan boils down his business philosophy to three premises, to which he passionately adheres:

220

First, *push the envelope*. A couple of examples. Over the past two years, Alan's been wrestling with this dilemma: How can we enable our customers (factories and machine shops) to choose most quickly and conveniently the best tool, best fluids, and best setup— at their timetable and convenience? An experience with Amazon.com gave him the idea to plunge into e-commerce at a scale unheard of in the industry. Now, by tapping into the vast Milacron Web site (www.milpro.com), a customer can use the Milacron search engines to determine the right product, to find the right salesperson or distributor, to put in an order, and to answer questions along the way. A myriad of hyper-links connect the customer to a full range of partners in the supply chain who can help the customer.

For the many customers who might want to see and feel the product rather than ordering through the Internet, the company launched its trademark "Milpro—Your Mobile Tool Crib." A nationwide fleet of small trucks goes right to the customer's facility on a regular basis, loaded with Milacron products, partners' products, a micro-coolant laboratory, and a computer for customized analysis and reports. The computer also ensures that each truck's inventory is tailored to the particular shops in the area it covers. Says Alan: "With our e-commerce and Milpro, our business is now speed and flexibility." Hmm . . . speed, flexibility . . . sound familiar?

Next, *share the credit*. One example will suffice: In early 1998, Dan Barron (a general manager, one of Alan's reports) proposed the mobile truck idea. Says Alan: "Wow, great idea," I said. "Okay. Do it." "Just like that?" gulped Dan. No bureaucratic delays? No boss's nitpicking? "Yeah, try it. Go build a couple trucks. See what product you can get in it. Find out what our customers want in it. Do the financials. You're running the show. Start now."

Says Alan: "You don't put a roadrunner in a 10 × 10 stall. If you look at the cartoons, the Road Runner always has a road to run on. My job is to help people build lots of roads, and then keep the roads clear of obstacles like boulders and corporate sacred cows."

Finally, *have fun doing it*. "I want everyone at Milacron to create exciting, neat projects where they can grow, contribute, take ownership, and enjoy what they do," says Alan. "That's fun. In fact, if you're not interested in having fun, I don't want to hire you. A few years ago, we landed a Harvard MBA who had been recruited by every company I can think of, including major consulting firms. He told me he took our offer because 'Alan, you're the only one who told me, if in six months you're not having more fun than you ever thought possible, I'll personally help you find another job.'"

What do you tell people in other companies who say, well, that a fun-loving culture may work for Milacron or Southwest Airlines, but it can't be done here? "I say, what a shame. *They've* closed the door on fun. *They've* decided that there's a policy that doesn't allow fun. Fun is how you keep your roadrunners motivated."

Smiling conspiratorially, he leans forward: "Here's another secret: Fun is how you turn the coyotes in your company into roadrunners!"

BY CHUCK JONES
CREATOR OF THE ROAD RUNNER
AND WILE E. COYOTE

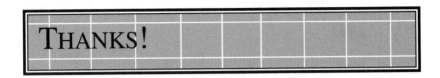

THANKS!

This is the page we use to say "thanks" to the many people who contributed to this book. We are struck by how insufficient the word *thanks* is for voicing our acknowledgment.

Thanks to . . .

- Larry Kirshbaum, President of Warner Books, for his belief that the business world had finally gotten loony enough to appreciate Looney Tunes.
- Rick Wolff of Warner Books for his leadership and guidance as our editor and friend.
- Michael Harkavy, Paula Allen, Victoria Selover, Charles Carney, and Allen Helbig of Warner Bros. for their enthusiasm for the project and great help with the layout.
- Jerry Price, whose Chromalloy Jet Engine Maintenance Conference in 1994 gave us the first forum to test the ideas that led to this book.
- Kathy Welton of IDG Books for early recognition of the potential of this book and for her great encouragement.
- Lloyd Rich, Peter Standish, and Eric Greenspan for their

important professional expertise and advice during the early phase of the effort.

- Ray Bard of Bard Books for his publishing expertise and network that helped facilitate our introduction to Warner Books.
- Gary Williams, Dean of the University of San Francisco School of Business, for creating a roadrunner environment in a highly challenging academic arena.
- Josh Engel and Bruce Taylor for yeoman's duty as our research assistants.
- Dina Andre of Chuck Jones Enterprises for her wonderful support on the original art.
- Leslie Stephen of Austin, Texas, for extraordinary editorial support.
- Ron Zemke and Tom Connellan of Performance Research Associates for their helpful feedback.
- Nancy Rainey Bell and Leslie Harari for their steadfast patience, special support, and never-ending love.

Finally, there is one person without whom this book would have never happened. He has been our "patron saint" and inspirational guide. Our special thanks to . . .

- Chuck Jones for his original illustration drawn just for this book and for his extraordinary genius in bringing to the world . . . Wile E. Coyote and the Road Runner.

NOTES

4   Lew Platt quote from "Lew Platt: Creating a Culture for Innovation" by John H. Sheridan, *Industry Week*, December 19, 1994, p. 26.

10 *Chuck Amuck* by Chuck Jones, NY: Farrar Straus & Giroux, 1989, p. 22; and *Chuck Reducks* by Chuck Jones, NY: Warner Books, 1996, p. 195.

13 "Are You on Digital Time?" by Alan M. Webber, *Fast Company*, February-March 1999, p. 116.

16 Thomas Friedman quote from *New York Times*, February 12, 1997.

27 "A Blueprint for Managing Change: A Conference Report," Joseph L. McCarthy (Editor) NY: The Conference Board, 1996.

27 Doug Ivester quote from *Wall Street Journal*, March 23, 1998, p. 12.

31 *Stewardship: Choosing Service Over Self-Interest* by Peter Block, San Francisco: Berrett-Koehler Publishers, 1993, p. 13.

37 *Jumping the Curve: Innovation and Strategic Choice in an Age of Transition* by Nicholas Imparato and Oren Harari, San Francisco: Jossey-Bass, 1994.

43 Scott Cook quote from *Fortune*, April 13, 1998, p. 152.

45 *One Size Fits One* by Gary Heil, Tom Parker, and Deborah C. Stephens, NY: John Wiley, 1997, p. 284.

51 The Charles Darwin Award is a public-domain contest sponsored annually by the Skyhawk Association, a fraternal-social affiliation of individuals who are fans of the A-4 Skyhawk aircraft. Their Web site is www.skyhawk.org.

64 *Net Worth: Shaping Markets When Customers Make the Rules,* by John Hagel and Marc Singer, Cambridge: Harvard Business School Press, 1999.
64 "Killer Apps" by Leigh Buchanan, *Inc.*, May 1998, p. 92.
64 Scott McNealy quote from *Business Week,* January 18, 1999, p. 67.
66 Quote by Bryan Burwell, *USA Today,* June 13, 1995, p. 10 C.
69 *The Trillion Dollar Enterprise* by Cyrus F. Freidheim, NY: Perseus Books, 1998.
92 AES story from "Power to the People" by Alex Markels, *Fast Company*, March 1998.
120 *Built to Last* by James Collins and Jerry Porras, NY: HarperBusiness, 1994.
123 *NPR Morning Edition* interview with John McElroy, January 29, 1999.
126 *Leadership Is an Art* by Max De Pree, NY: Doubleday, 1989, p. 9.
139 *The Roadrunner in Fact and Folk-Lore* by J. Frank Dobie, Austin: Texas Folk-Lore Society, 1939, p. 27.
141 *Chuck Amuck* by Chuck Jones, p. 225.
144 *Nuts! Southwest Airlines' Crazy Recipe for Business and Personal Success* by Kevin and Jackie Freiberg, Austin: Bard Books, 1996, p. 130.
148 *The Corporate Mystic* by Gay Hendricks and Kate Ludeman, NY: Bantam Books, 1996, p. 45.
149 Tom Peters quote from *Executive Excellence,* January 1998, p. 20.
154 "America's Most Admired Companies," *Fortune,* March 1, 1999, p. F-4.
160 Reference to Bain and Company and Ernst & Young from "What's Your Strategy for Managing Knowledge" by Morten T. Hansen, Nitin Nohria, and Thomas Tierney, *Harvard Business Review*, March-April 1999, p. 113.
162 Al Gore story from *Nuts!* by Kevin and Jackie Freiberg, p. 129.
163 Dayton Hudson story from "Mass with Class" by Michelle Colin, *Forbes,* January 11, 1999.
166 Michael Eisner quote from *Executive Excellence,* January 1998, p. 4.
167 Santayana line from *Chuck Amuck* by Chuck Jones, p. 222.
167 "My Biggest Mistake" by Andy Grove, *Inc.*, May 1998, p. 117.
170 *The Fifth Discipline* by Peter Senge, NY: Doubleday, 1990.
180 *Road-Runner!* by Virginia Douglas, Happy Camp, CA: Naturegraph Publishers, 1984.
181 "Strategy As Revolution" by Gary Hamel and C.K. Prahalad, *Harvard Business Review,* June-July 1996, p. 122.
188 *High Velocity Culture Change: A Handbook for Managers* by Price Pritchett and Ron Pound, Dallas: Pritchett Publishing, 1993, p. 39.
188 Alfonso Roma story from *Wall Street Journal,* January 29, 1999.

192 "America's Most Admired Corporations" by Anne Fisher, *Fortune,*
     October 27, 1997.

203 Accountemps survey from *HR Focus,* February 1993.

203 Average workweek reference from *USA Today,* March 1, 1998.

203 Digital Equipment reference from *301 Ways to Have Fun at Work*
     by Dave Hemsath and Leslie Yerkes, San Francisco: Berrett-
     Koehler, 1997, p. ix.

203 Colorado Health Sciences study from *301 Ways* by Dave Hemsath
     and Leslie Yerkes, p. ix.

203 More free time study from *Barron's,* March 9, 1998, p. 33.

204 Description of Richard Branson from *Esquire* by Julie Baumgold,
     August 1996, pp. 131–132.

204 "Is Herb Kelleher America's Best CEO?" by Kenneth Labich,
     Fortune, May 2, 1994.

206 Sports quotes from Delta *Sky* magazine, February 1998.

212 Monster Board story from "Monster Board Has Fun" by Cathy
     Olofson, *Fast Company,* August 1998.

215 "The Bill and Warren Show" by Brent Schlender, *Fortune,* July 20,
     1998.

216 *Fortune* cover, March 16, 1998.

INDEX

Index

INDEX

Index

INDEX

Index

INDEX

Index

INDEX

Index

INDEX

Index

ABOUT THE AUTHORS

Chip R. Bell is a senior partner with Performance Research Associates and manages their Dallas, Texas, office. Prior to starting a consulting firm in the late 1970s, he was Vice President and Director of Management and Organization Development for NCNB (now BankAmerica). He is the author or co-author of eleven books, including: *Customers As Partners, Managers As Mentors, Managing Knock Your Socks Off Service* (with Ron Zemke), and *Dance Lessons: Six Steps to Great Partnerships in Business and Life* (with Heather Shea). Dr. Bell has been hired to hunt down coyotes in several Fortune 500 companies, including IBM, Cadillac, USAA, Microsoft, Lucent Technologies, MCI WorldCom, Lockheed Martin, Harley-Davidson, Marriott, 3M, Nortel, Merrill Lynch, Ritz-Carlton, Morgan Stanley Dean Witter, and Victoria's Secret. One of Chip's personal goals is to set the State of Texas record for the largest catfish caught on a cane pole. He resides in Dallas.

Chip R. Bell
Performance Research Associates, Inc.
25 Highland Park #100
Dallas, Texas 75205-2785
214/522-5777

Oren Harari is Professor of Management at the University of San Francisco, the author of the best-selling 1999 book *Leapfrogging the Competition,* and the co-author of *Jumping the Curve,* rated by *Library Journal* as one of the top forty business books of 1994. He writes a monthly international column, "Harari at Large," for *Management Review* and is the first designated "management expert" on *Time* magazine's interactive Time Vista Web site. From 1984 to 1996, he served as a senior consultant with the Tom Peters Group and was one of its most requested speakers. Dr. Harari's work as a speaker, consultant, and author incorporates cutting-edge material on competitive advantage, organizational change, and transformational leadership. His clients have included such major organizations as MCI WorldCom, Dell Computer, Merck, 3M, IBM, Cisco Systems, Citibank, Xerox, Fidelity Investments, and Toyota U.S.A. One of Oren's personal goals is to start another rock band and play in honky-tonks all around Northern California. He resides in the San Francisco Bay Area.

Oren Harari
McLaren School of Business
University of San Francisco
2130 Fulton Avenue
San Francisco, California 94960
415/459-2345 or 422-6277